The Industrial Revolution

AMERICAN HISTORY

The Industrial Revolution

Kevin Hillstrom

LUCENT BOOKS
A part of Gale, Cengage Learning

GALE
CENGAGE Learning™

Detroit • New York • San Francisco • New Haven, Conn • Waterville, Maine • London

© 2009 Gale, Cengage Learning

ALL RIGHTS RESERVED. No part of this work covered by the copyright herein may be reproduced, transmitted, stored, or used in any form or by any means graphic, electronic, or mechanical, including but not limited to photocopying, recording, scanning, digitizing, taping, Web distribution, information networks, or information storage and retrieval systems, except as permitted under Section 107 or 108 of the 1976 United States Copyright Act, without the prior written permission of the publisher.

Every effort has been made to trace the owners of copyrighted material.

LIBRARY OF CONGRESS CATALOGING-IN-PUBLICATION DATA
Hillstrom, Kevin, 1963–
Industrial revolution / by Kevin Hillstrom.
p. cm. — (American history)
Includes bibliographical references and index.
ISBN 978-1-4205-0066-0 (hardcover)
1. Industrial revolution—United States—Juvenile literature. I. Title.
HC105.H654 2009
330.973'08--dc22
2008027342

Lucent Books
27500 Drake Rd
Farmington Hills MI 48331

ISBN-13: 978-1-4205-0066-0
ISBN-10: 1-4205-0066-X

Printed in the United States of America
2 3 4 5 6 7 12 11 10 09

Contents

Foreword

The United States has existed as a nation for just over 200 years. By comparison, Rome existed as a nation-state for more than 1000 years. Out of a few struggling British colonies, the United States developed relatively quickly into a world power whose policy decisions and culture have great influence on the world stage. What events and aspirations drove this young American nation to such great heights in such a short period of time? The answer lies in a close study of its varied and unique history. As James Baldwin once remarked, "American history is longer, larger, more various, more beautiful, and more terrible than anything anyone has ever said about it."

The basic facts of United States history—names, dates, places, battles, treaties, speeches, and acts of Congress—fill countless textbooks. These facts, though essential to a thorough understanding of world events, are rarely compelling for students. More compelling are the stories in history, the experience of history.

Titles in this series explore the history of the country and the experiences of Americans. What influences led the colonists to risk everything and break from Britain? Who was the driving force behind the Constitution? Which factors led thousands of people to leave their homelands and settle in the United States? Questions like these do not have simple answers; by discussing them, however, we can view the past as a more real, interesting, and accessible place.

Students will find excellent tools for research and investigation in every title. Lucent Books' American History series provides not only facts, but also the analysis and context necessary for insightful critical thinking about history and about current events. Fully cited quotations from historical figures, eyewitnesses, letters, speeches, and writings bring vibrancy and authority to the text. Annotated bibliographies allow students to evaluate and locate sources for further investigation. Sidebars highlight important and interesting figures, events, or related primary source excerpts. Timelines, maps, and full color images add another dimension of accessibility to the stories being told.

It has been said the past has a history of repeating itself, for good and ill. In these pages, students will learn a bit about both and, perhaps, better understand their own place in this world.

Important Dates at the Time of

1776
The American colonies declare their independence from England.

1787
America's founding fathers open the Constitutional Convention in Philadelphia.

1807
Robert Fulton makes his famous steamboat journey up and down the Hudson River.

1825
The Erie Canal opens for business.

1844
Samuel Morse unveils the first working telegraph.

1886
The American Federation of Labor, the most influential labor union in U.S. history, is founded.

1770 1780 1790 1800 1810 1820 1830 1840 1850 1860 1870 1880

1852
Massachusetts passes the nation's first mandatory school attendance laws.

1861
The Civil War begins.

1870
John D. Rockefeller establishes the Standard Oil Company.

1863
President Abraham Lincoln issues the Emancipation Proclamation.

1865
The Civil War ends with a Northern victory; President Lincoln is assassinated.

of the Industrial Revolution

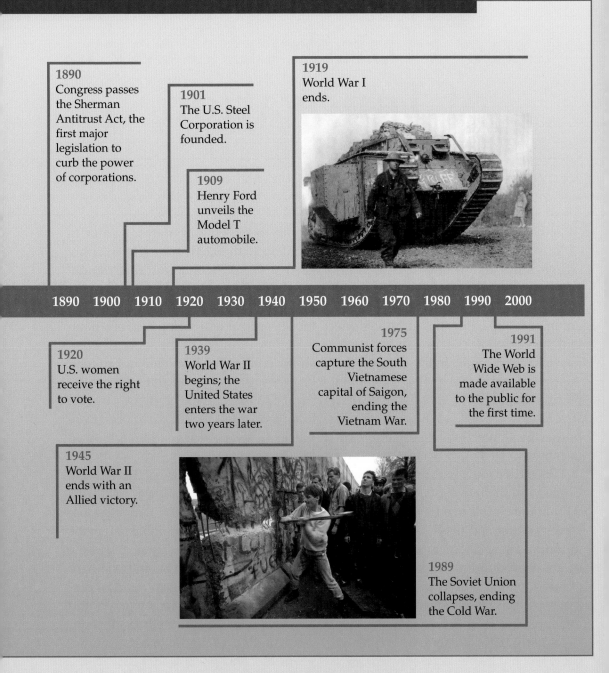

1890
Congress passes the Sherman Antitrust Act, the first major legislation to curb the power of corporations.

1901
The U.S. Steel Corporation is founded.

1909
Henry Ford unveils the Model T automobile.

1919
World War I ends.

1890 1900 1910 1920 1930 1940 1950 1960 1970 1980 1990 2000

1920
U.S. women receive the right to vote.

1939
World War II begins; the United States enters the war two years later.

1975
Communist forces capture the South Vietnamese capital of Saigon, ending the Vietnam War.

1991
The World Wide Web is made available to the public for the first time.

1945
World War II ends with an Allied victory.

1989
The Soviet Union collapses, ending the Cold War.

Introduction

One Hundred Years of Innovation

In the space of a single century, the industrial revolution ushered in new machines and technology, rich new sources of energy, and lucrative new forms of business and commerce. The combined impact of these innovations laid the groundwork for modern society as we know it today. In the process, the Age of Industrialization lifted the United States—home to the most spectacular successes of the era—to its present position as the planet's leading economic superpower.

The industrial revolution began in England in the late eighteenth century. At that time, motorized machines powered by water and fossil fuels were first introduced as an alternative to traditional means of production, which had been dependent on the muscle of humans and livestock. This revolution in manufacturing spread into other European nations in the early 1800s. But its greatest impact came when it leaped across the Atlantic Ocean to the United States, a country bursting with hardy immigrants, entrepreneurial spirit, and bountiful natural resources. The marriage of these potent elements changed America from a mostly agricultural society into one dominated by industry in the space of a few short decades. The economic and cultural heartbeat of the nation shifted from the rural countryside to the chaotic but vibrant industrial cities that had been mere villages a few decades earlier. American life changed forever.

The first great industry of this new era was the textile industry. It was in the textile mills of New England that large machines first became an essential part of the manufacturing process. These mills were also the first American businesses to introduce the "factory system" of mass production. Under this system, workers and large machines were brought together under a single roof, and workers were responsible for specialized tasks in the

A young girl stands in front of a power loom in a Vermont textile mill. This industry became an essential part of the industrial revolution.

production process. This mode of manufacturing, which took the production of goods out of individual homes and workshops, quickly spread to other industries.

As the nineteenth century unfolded, new technological breakthroughs, new methods of distribution and management, and the ambitions of wealthy investors all combined to bring about a wave of entirely new industries. Railroads and steamships chugged across the American landscape, giving farmers, ranchers, manufacturers, and retailers access to markets that lay hundreds of miles away. Steel foundries and oil refineries roared to life, providing vital materials and energy for the creation and operation of both massive factories and the sprawling cities those factories inhabited. And by the dawn of the twentieth century, amazing inventions like the telephone and the automobile were poised to make their own enduring imprints on American society and business.

The astonishing economic impact of the industrial revolution, though, was fully matched by its influence on American culture and identity. The wealth it generated gave the United States the ability to conquer and settle the American West, thus extending its borders all the way to the Pacific Ocean. The economic opportunities found in the factories and mills convinced millions of immigrants from Europe and other parts of the world to make their home in America. And the inventors and engineers that the revolution created brought electrical lighting, indoor plumbing, and other new material comforts to American families. The industrial revolution also gave Americans the means to discover—through travel or newspaper reading—distant parts of the country that would have remained complete mysteries to previous generations. Finally, the Age of Industrialization changed the United States' relationship with the rest of the world. It transformed America into a formidable military power and the planet's leading source of wheat, cotton, coal, oil, and numerous other vital goods by the early twentieth century. As one scholar observes, "The industrial revolution constituted one of those rare occasions in world history when the human species altered its framework of existence."[1]

These benefits, however, did not mask the massive social and economic turmoil that the industrial revolution also brought to America. As the nineteenth century progressed, industrial cities became overcrowded and riddled with political corruption, and many urban neighborhoods deteriorated into slums. Corporation owners exploited workers—including children—who toiled long hours under hazardous conditions for meager pay. Large swaths of publicly owned wilderness were sacrificed to the banks, mining companies, railroads, and logging corporations that dominated the nation's economy. And the fierce battle for economic advancement, played out on factory floors and in mining camps from the Atlantic states to California, sparked ugly bouts of ethnic and racial discrimination and violence.

The industrial revolution even gave new life to slavery, an institution that had

Cotton is readied for transportation from Atlanta, Georgia, to the northern states in 1880. The mechanization of the industrial revolution gave new life to the cotton industry of the South.

been in decline. The mechanization of cotton production gave the Deep South a huge economic incentive to keep African Americans enslaved. Without slaves to scour the cotton fields, the machines that had made "King Cotton" the most lucrative crop in the world would lie idle and the Southern economy would fall apart. The Southern states thus charted a collision course with their Northern neighbors that ended with the American Civil War, which ripped across the nation from 1861 to 1865.

By the close of the nineteenth century, many Americans felt that the fast-paced new world in which they now lived was eroding the nation's vitality and moral character. "A sense of injustice [had become] part of the new glittering, gaudy machine age," says one critic. "Machines of steel and copper and wood and stone, and bookkeeping and managerial talent, were creating a new order. It looked glamorous. It seemed permanent; yet . . . discontent rose in the hearts of the people."[2]

Efforts to address this discontent took many forms in the twentieth century, from social reform movements to increased government regulation. But significant sectors of the American public—especially those who were thriving in the new economy—opposed these measures as un-American or antibusiness. This philosophical battle continues to rage today.

In the meantime, the economic, social, and entrepreneurial forces unleashed by the industrial revolution continue to shape the course of American lives. U.S. citizens now live in an era in which the Internet, orbiting communication satellites, sleek automobiles, sophisticated home appliances, and nuclear submarines are all taken for granted. Yet none of these spectacular technological achievements might have come to pass—at least in the form they take today—were it not for the ambitious inventors and bold entrepreneurs who first brought the industrial revolution to life.

Chapter One

The Birthplace of the Industrial Revolution

Decades before industrialization began to make its mark in the United States, the age of mechanization and mass production took root in England. It was there that the first factories of mass production were opened, and it was also there that some of the most important inventions of the industrial revolution—most notably the steam engine—were introduced. But the full promise of these industrial schemes and inventions was not fulfilled until they were exported to America, where they became the foundation for a stunning era of economic and social transformation.

Textiles—The First Modern Industry

The nation of England—along with Wales and Scotland—occupies the North Atlantic island of Great Britain, just off the northern coast of western Europe. In many ways, the England that existed in the eighteenth century provided fertile territory for the birth of the industrial revolution. The country was blessed with a stable government, a thriving agriculture-oriented economy, a sophisticated banking system, and a culture that encouraged business enterprise. England was sometimes described as a nation of shopkeepers, and this was meant as a compliment. But England was also a nation of investors, which proved to be a critical element in the early days of industrialization. These wealthy investors were constantly on the alert for new business opportunities, and in the mid-1700s a series of events in the nation's modest world of textile manufacturing began to catch their eye.

Traditionally, the English textile industry had been a home-based one in which individual workers took small amounts of fabrics to their respective homes or shops, created garments, blankets, and other goods on a "piecework" basis, and then returned the finished product to the

The spinning jenny, invented by James Hargreaves, was the first automated process for spinning cotton into yarn.

manufacturer in exchange for modest compensation. Most of the textiles created under this system were made from wool rather than cotton. In fact, cotton was viewed as a luxury fabric because the natural twist in its fibers made it very labor-intensive to produce.

In the mid-eighteenth century, however, a flurry of inventions forever changed the way that English textiles were made. The first of these important inventions was the flying shuttle, which was unveiled by John Kay in 1733. This innovation to the loom dramatically increased the speed at which cotton threads could be woven into cloth. This milestone

was followed three decades later by the introduction of the spinning jenny, created by James Hargreaves, and the spinning frame, invented by wigmaker Richard Arkwright. The latter machine was particularly important because it gave textile makers the first automated process for spinning cotton yarn. With Arkwright's invention, quality clothing and other textiles could be made quickly and inexpensively with cotton, which not surprisingly became much more popular with both manufacturers and consumers.

The spinning frame—which later became known as the water frame when Arkwright adjusted his invention so that it could be powered by water rather than by hand—made its inventor a very rich man. Gathering investors to his side, Arkwright built a massive cotton mill in Derbyshire, on the banks of the Derwent River, and watched the money pour in. "Arkwright lived the life of a feudal lord," writes one scholar. "The mill was his castle, as carefully guarded as any fortress. . . . He played the lord of the manor to the hilt, handing out annual prizes to the butchers, bakers, and grocers whom he considered had best served the town."[3] Arkwright established several other water-powered textile mills as well, and these operations are today widely regarded as early examples of the modern industrial factory system.

"Cottonopolis" and Other English Textile Centers

Arkwright was hardly the only Englishman to build a fortune out of cotton in the eighteenth century, however. The exciting changes in textile manufacturing wrought by the spinning jenny, the water frame, and the power loom (invented by the Reverend Edmund Cartwright in 1785) convinced numerous investors to become involved in the industry. Many areas of England, such as the county of Lancashire, experienced an explosion of textile factory construction during the 1770s and 1780s, especially along rivers that could turn the waterwheels of the new mill designs. Once these factories were built, the owners had no trouble

Defining England, Great Britain, and the United Kingdom

The nations of England, Wales, and Scotland occupy the North Atlantic island of Great Britain, just off the northern coast of western Europe. Together, these three states and the province of Northern Ireland (which is located on the neighboring island of Ireland) comprise the country known as the United Kingdom (UK). England is the largest and most heavily populated of the UK's four constituent countries.

The United Kingdom of Great Britain was founded in 1707 by an Act of Union that united the three states into one country with a single Parliament (although Scotland has always retained its own legal system). Nearly one hundred years later, in 1801, a new Act of Union joined the neighboring island nation of Ireland to Great Britain. At this point, the full name of the country became the United Kingdom of Great Britain and Ireland. In 1921, however, the Republic of Ireland, which held the majority of the island territory, became independent. Only Northern Ireland remained part of the United Kingdom, so the full name changed to what it is today—the United Kingdom of Great Britain and Northern Ireland.

rustling up orders for their products. "Cotton cloth production increased dramatically," confirms one economic historian. "In 1765 about five hundred thousand pounds of cotton was spun into thread in Britain, almost all of it at home. Twenty years later sixteen million pounds were spun, mostly in factories."[4]

At times it seemed that nothing could slow the flood of wealth being generated at these textile mills. Public demand for inexpensive cotton clothing and other materials continued to surge in the early 1800s. The industry was able to meet this demand because it could draw on the large cotton crops generated in India, which was an English colony at the time.

In addition, England had large reserves of coal, so when the steam engine replaced water power in the early 1800s, the country's textile makers did not miss a beat.

By the dawn of the nineteenth century, Manchester and other English cities had become the world's leading centers for the manufacture of textiles. Manchester, in fact, had acquired the nickname "Cottonopolis," a tribute to its importance to the global cotton trade. But in the process, the textile centers of England also became the first cities in the world to experience the dark side of industrial mass production.

Many mill owners in the United Kingdom ruthlessly exploited the workforce

Women operate looms in a Lancashire cotton mill. Lancashire experienced an explosion of textile factory construction during the 1770s and 1780s.

in their quest for riches. Long hours and hazardous working conditions were the rule rather than the exception for the men, women, and children who toiled in their factories. One Manchester physician, J.P. Kay, expressed outright horror at the situation: "Whilst the engine runs, the people must work—men, women and children yoked together with iron and steam," he lamented. "[The human body, which is] breakable in the best case, is chained fast to the iron machine, which knows no suffering and no weariness."[5] Another observer stated that the textile factories had changed all of Lancashire from a "green and pleasant land" into a "sordid blackened squalidness."[6]

James Watt's steam engine allowed owners the ability to build their factories far from rivers and, as a result, expand their production capacity.

Such complaints did not convince English factory owners or government officials to address the problems of industrial pollution, child labor, or worker exploitation. But they did bring about the birth of the first social reform movements dedicated to combating the darker aspects of industrialization.

The Steam Engine

The second major development in England's industrial revolution occurred in 1765, when a Scottish maker of mathematical instruments named James Watt unveiled an innovative new steam engine that could be used for a wide range of industrial purposes.

Watt's invention marked the end of a long quest by European inventors to harness steam for human use. In fact, early experiments in steam power were made in Europe as far back as the 1600s. Not much came of these efforts, though, until 1705, when an English blacksmith named Thomas Newcomen produced a primitive engine that was powered by steam. Within a few decades, steam-powered pumps based on Newcomen's design were being widely used to remove water from English coal-mining pits.

The steam engine design unveiled by Watt was based on Newcomen's engine,

James Watt and the Age of Steam

Born in Scotland's Clyde River valley in January 1736, James Watt established a thriving mathematical instrument repair shop in Glasgow as a young man. In the early 1760s he began working on improvements to the steam engine design created by Thomas Newcomen more than a half-century earlier. By 1769 Watt had a patent for his improved design, and a few years later he entered into a long and profitable partnership with industrialist Matthew Boulton.

During the 1780s and 1790s Watt made a series of improvements to his steam engine designs, and all of these improvements eventually found their way into the factories and mines of England. Early in the nineteenth century, Watt steam engines also were exported to the United States in significant numbers. Over time, American engineers built on Watt's work to utilize steam as a means to power steamboats and railroads that became an essential part of the industrial revolution in the United States in the nineteenth century.

Watt retired in 1800, but he continued to tinker with inventions, including a new type of oil lamp. He also traveled widely throughout western Europe, and even bought an estate in Wales. He died on August 19, 1819, in England.

---

but it was far more efficient and sophisticated. Most important, it could be easily modified for use in the Lancashire textile mills. The arrival of Watt's steam engine, which was fueled by coal, freed mill owners from having to locate their facilities on the banks of rivers and streams. Textile factories soon roared to life in regions of England that were far from any river current, and existing mills that invested in the new steam technology were able to expand their production capacity dramatically.

The arrival of this new steam technology also sparked economic growth and innovation in other industries across England. In the nation's ironworks, for example, the introduction of steam-powered bellows in blast furnaces helped iron makers switch over from charcoal to coke, an inexpensive byproduct of coal. These coke-fired forges generated higher temperatures than charcoal, which enabled ironmasters to burn off a greater percentage of carbon and produce iron products of greater strength and durability. Steam power also liberated flour mills from England to Wales from the necessity of building and operating next to waterways. Finally, steam engines became the centerpiece of efforts to make an exciting new mode of transportation called the railroad more efficient and effective. By the 1820s steam-powered railways were emerging as an important method of transporting coal—the fuel of industrialization—and other goods to cities and factories in many parts of the United Kingdom.

English Factories and American Ingenuity

One of the most remarkable aspects of the emergence of an industrial revolution in England was that it unfolded around the same time that the British lost their most prized foreign possession— the colonies in North America—in the American War for Independence. The successful colonial rebellion that resulted in the establishment of the United States of America in 1776 angered the British people. But it did not blind them to the potential economic benefits of trade with their former subjects, especially after a young American inventor named Eli Whitney came up with an amazing new invention that turned the textile industry upside down.

A native New Englander, Whitney had only recently graduated from Yale University when he paid a visit to a friend who managed a cotton plantation in Georgia in 1792. During his time in Georgia, he became intrigued by one of the most vexing problems confronting cotton growers in the South. "I have . . . heard much said of the extreme difficulty of ginning [separating seeds from cotton fibers]," he wrote to his father. "There were a number of respectable Gentlemen . . . who all agreed that if a machine could be invented which would clean the cotton with expedition, it would be a great

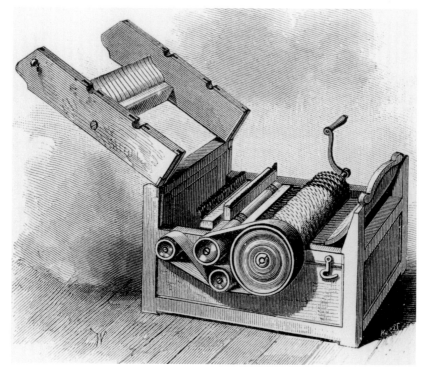

With the invention of Eli Whitney's cotton gin, the United States became one of the world's leading producers of cotton during the 1800s.

thing both to the country and the inventor. . . . I involuntarily happened to be thinking on the subject and struck out a plan for a machine in my mind."[7]

Whitney worked diligently on his invention for the next several months, and in 1794 he patented his cotton gin. "The machine was simplicity itself," says one scholar.

Whitney studded a roller with nails, set half an inch apart. When the roller was turned, the nails passed through a grid, pulling the cotton lint from below through the grid, but leaving the seeds behind. A rotating brush swept the lint off the nails into a compartment while the seeds fell into a separate compartment. With Whitney's cotton gin, a laborer could do in a single day what had taken twenty-five laborers to do in that amount of time before.[8]

When southern planters saw Whitney's cotton gin in action, they rushed to place orders. Within a matter of a few years, the impact of the invention could be seen throughout the South. In 1793 the United States produced about 5 million pounds (2,268t) of cotton, less than 1 percent of the world's total cotton crop (the leading producer at this time was India,

Eli Whitney and the Cotton Boom

Eli Whitney was born in Westborough, Massachusetts, on December 8, 1765. After graduating from Yale University in 1792, he went to Georgia, where he was inspired to devise a machine to help cotton planters easily separate cotton seeds from the balls of fiber. His "cotton gin"—essentially a mechanical device composed of a rotating metal cylinder with teeth and separate compartments for seeds and cotton—provided an enormous boost to American cotton growers. However, it also led the Deep South to become even more deeply wedded to its slave-dependent agricultural economy throughout the first half of the nineteenth century.

Whitney hoped to use his cotton gin patent to make himself a wealthy man, but these efforts failed. Patent laws in the United States in the 1790s were weak and rarely enforced, and his cotton gin design was so simple that any skilled craftsman could make one. In the late 1790s and early 1800s, though, he became a successful gun manufacturer. In fact, his gun-making operations introduced the concept of interchangeable parts—triggers and other parts that could be used in multiple models rather than just one product type—to American manufacturing. Whitney died in New Haven, Connecticut, on January 8, 1825.

a British colony). By the first decade of the nineteenth century, though, the cotton gin had pushed annual American cotton production up to 40 million pounds (18,144t). U.S. production continued to surge in the 1810s and 1820s, and by 1830 American planters were producing about half of the world's cotton.[9] All told, cotton production in the United States rose from about 100,000 bales in 1800 to 2.13 million bales by 1850.

Slavery Makes a Comeback

This enormous leap in cotton production would never have occurred if there had not been a market for southern cotton. The "Cottonopolis" factories and the other textile centers of England, though, clamored to acquire every boll of cotton that the Deep South could squeeze out of the ground. This demand was a great financial boon to planters. But it also breathed new life into slavery, which had been fading—both in importance and in practice—across most of America for much of the late eighteenth century. "Cotton changed all that," reported one historian. "After 1793 the price of a slave racheted upward. An institution that had been in steep decline suddenly became an important part of the economic equation for Southern farmers eager to fulfill England's ravenous demand for cotton."[10]

With each passing year, the cotton-based economy of the American South became more deeply intertwined with slavery. For example, in addition to being a major *exporter* of cotton, the South of the early nineteenth century became a major *importer* of manufactured goods, since it did not invest much in the factories that produced such goods. This state of affairs made the South a fierce critic of high tariffs—taxes—on goods received from overseas. The North, on the other hand, was industrializing quickly, so that region of the country favored high tariffs to protect domestic manufacturers.

These clashes, however, paled next to the divide between North and South on the issue of slavery. The North-based abolitionist movement condemned slavery as a great moral evil, but many white southerners viewed calls to end slavery as a mortal threat to their economy and their way of life. And the importance of cotton to the overall U.S. economy led some southerners to conclude that the North would never try to forcibly end slavery in America. "The slaveholding South is now the controlling power of the world," declared South Carolina senator James H. Hammond in 1858. "Nobody on earth dares . . . to make war on cotton. Cotton is king."[11]

Across the Atlantic Ocean, though, observers in England watched the growing tensions between North and South with alarm. "The lives of nearly two millions of our countrymen are dependent upon the cotton crops of America," wrote the editors of a British magazine called *The Economist* in 1855. "Should any dire calamity befall the land of cotton, a thousand of our merchant ships would rot idly in dock; ten thousand mills must stop their busy looms; two thousand thousand mouths would starve, for lack of food to feed them."[12]

Industrialization Reaches American Shores

At the start of the nineteenth century, England's textile centers and its other mechanized industries were the envy of the rest of the world. With this in mind, British lawmakers tried to preserve their country's economic advantage over the United States and other nations by passing laws that prohibited the export of textile machinery and textile-related "intellectual property" (creations of the mind with potential economic value, such as inventions, industrial engineering designs, and artistic and literary works). They were determined to keep the economic benefits of mechanization to themselves for as long as possible.

These efforts to keep industrialization within British borders were doomed to fail, though. For one thing, Americans were determined to build a country that was not dependent on England or any other foreign nation for its economic health and vitality. "Long before Eli Whitney and before the first muskets were drawn at Concord in 1776 [at the start of the U.S. Revolutionary War], the eventual leaders of the new republic realized that to be self-sustaining our citizens would have to dress themselves in native cloth grown and manufactured with-

out any reliance on foreign powers,"[13] writes one American scholar.

Perhaps even more important, the potential for riches was simply too great to keep some ambitious entrepreneurs from

British immigrant Samuel Slater opened the first U.S. industrial textile mill in 1790. Many historians regard this event as the beginning of America's industrial revolution.

figuring out ways to bring England's textile machinery to American shores. In 1790 British immigrant Samuel Slater opened America's first industrial textile mill in America after completing an apprenticeship at a textile factory in England. The mill was a testament to Slater's powers of memorization, for it duplicated virtually every aspect of British textile operations and technology. Today, many economic historians regard the opening of Slater's textile mill as the beginning of America's industrial revolution.

Slater's factory was a milestone in American economic history, but an even more prominent figure in U.S. textiles emerged two decades later. In 1812 Massachusetts native Francis Cabot Lowell returned to the United States from a two-year stay in England. During his visits to Manchester and other industrial centers, Lowell had committed many aspects of their rapidly evolving textile operations to memory. Armed with this knowledge, Lowell built textile mills in Waltham, Massachusetts, that integrated all aspects of the cotton manufacturing process—even the dyeing of cloth—under one roof. By the end of the decade, the Waltham mills had grown into America's first corporate empire, and the industrial factory system that had transformed England was firmly entrenched in the U.S. business world.

Chapter Two

The Industrial Age Transforms America

Within a few years after the industrial revolution first stirred to life in the United States in the early nineteenth century, big machines, ingenious inventions, and new ways of doing business were transforming American life and commerce in spectacular ways. This enormous rate of industrial growth was due to several important factors. First, America was home to a wide assortment of talented and ambitious inventors and entrepreneurs, as well as a fast-growing workforce that could fill its new factories. In addition, the young nation possessed an economic system—capitalism—that encouraged investment and business enterprise. Finally, the United States had an incredible reservoir of natural resources to draw on, including rivers deep and wide enough for ships to navigate, huge reserves of coal and other valuable minerals, vast stands of timber, and thousands of miles of fertile farmland. These raw materials gave early American engineers, inventors, and corporate executives the power to make their dreams of industrialization become a reality during the first half of the nineteenth century.

Facing the Industrial Age with Confidence

In England industrialization had been greeted with distrust and resistance in significant parts of the country. Many British people liked their traditional ways of life, and they feared the impact of mechanization on their jobs and families. These fears about industrialization became even more intense after stories filtered out about the working conditions that evolved in Manchester and other early textile manufacturing centers. By the early nineteenth century, in fact, English textile workers known as Luddites had even organized violent protests against the mechanized textile mills.

In the United States, though, machines and factories and steam power were usually welcomed with open arms. Farmers and city workers alike were happy to have machines that could make their work less exhausting, and business leaders embraced any tool that could increase the output and efficiency of their operations. American consumers also welcomed the promise of greater selection and availability of goods. Lawmakers and community leaders were similarly enthusiastic, for they shared the wide-spread American belief that their new nation was destined for great things. To many people the industrial revolution seemed like the means by which America would begin charting its course to greatness.

This welcoming attitude came in large measure from the fact that the structure of American society was ideally suited to welcome industrialization. Mechanization and other hallmarks of industrialization

A Luddite mob rioting in the nineteenth century because they felt their jobs were in jeopardy due to the mechanization of the textile mills.

were instantly recognized as keys to greater wealth—which was the most common measuring stick of success in the United States. Talented entrepreneurs and engineers thus flocked to various newly mechanized industries.

Finally, the industrialization of American business was aided by the fact that events in England had already *proved* that machines could improve productivity and profitability. American business leaders knew that industrialization was the wave of the future, and legislators at both the state and federal levels did everything in their power to pave the way for investment in industrial machinery and processes. They could also easily draw on the knowledge of British engineers and managers with firsthand experience with the industrialization process. After all, American entrepreneurs and British engineers shared a common language. This made it much easier for U.S. firms to implement the industrial knowledge contained between the covers of British trade manuals and inside the heads of British engineers that they were able to lure to America from England.

A Revolution in Transportation

Early American industrialism was centered in the northeastern states, where most of the nation's population was concentrated in the early 1800s. The metro-

The development of the Erie Canal locks at Lockport, New York, in the late nineteenth century had a tremendous economic impact on the United States.

politan centers of this region—cities like Boston, New York, and Philadelphia—not only had lots of workers on hand but also supported banks and other major sources of investment capital. In addition, all of these cities had access to major navigable waterways such as rivers, lakes, and the ocean.

The existence of such waterways was a huge factor in the economic prospects of any early-nineteenth-century American city. First of all, rivers such as the Hudson, Connecticut, Potomac, James, and Susquehanna provided vital water power for New England's early textile mills. But as time passed and steam power supplanted water power in American factories, the other value of these waterways—as transportation routes—was spotlighted. Major roadway networks were nonexistent at the time, and commercially viable railroads had not even been invented yet, so rivers, lakes, and coastal waters served as the highways of the nation during the first half century of its existence. New York, for example, became an early center of shipping, banking, and industry because it was built at the juncture of a deep Atlantic harbor and the mighty Hudson River. At the southern end of the country, the same resources—a deep ocean bay and a great river (the Mississippi)—accounted for the emergence of New Orleans as the South's leading center of trade.

In the 1810s and 1820s American legislators and business interests tried to make the nation's water-based transportation system more effective by adding on to it with massive canals. These man-made waterways were designed to connect potential farming regions and other landlocked areas of the American interior, as well as existing waterways, with other river and lake transportation systems.

The first and greatest of these massive canal projects was the Erie Canal in New York State. Construction on the canal began in 1817, when the New York legislature finally authorized the project after years of lobbying from supporters such as De Witt Clinton, a politician who served New York as a U.S. senator, governor, and mayor of New York City. The Erie Canal, vowed Clinton, would "convey more riches on its waters than any other canal in the world," releasing financial resources "to be expanded in great public improvements; in encouraging the arts and sciences; in patronizing the operations of industry; in fostering the inventions of genius, and in diffusing the blessing of knowledge."[14]

In 1925—eight years after the massive project broke ground—the Erie Canal's surveyors, engineers, and laborers finally completed their work. The finished canal stretched 363 miles (584km) from the cities of Albany (on the lower reaches of the Hudson River) to Buffalo (on the shores of Lake Erie). As champions such as Clinton had predicted, the canal had an enormous economic impact on the United States. It opened a tremendously lucrative trade link between eastern population centers such as New York City and the territories of the Great Lakes region. Eastbound shipments of Great

De Witt Clinton and His Famous "Ditch"

One of the political giants of New York State, De Witt Clinton also is known as the father of the Erie Canal. Clinton was born on March 2, 1769, in Napanoch, New York. His uncle was George Clinton, who was the first governor of New York and served as vice president of the United States from 1805 to 1812.

De Witt Clinton spent virtually his entire adult life in politics. In 1798 he became a member of the New York State Assembly, and he spent the next several years rising through the ranks of state legislators. In 1802 he was elected to the United States Senate, but he spent only two years in that capacity before beginning a twelve-year stint as mayor of New York City. Midway through his tenure as mayor, he ran for president of the United States as the candidate of the Federalist Party, but he was defeated by President James Madison.

During his many years as mayor of New York, Clinton became best known as the driving force behind the campaign to build a canal that would connect the Hudson River to Lake Erie. Some critics ridiculed the proposed canal as "Clinton's Ditch," but legislative and public support for the project was strong. Thanks to Clinton's tireless advocacy for the project, work on the canal began in 1817. When it was completed in 1825, the Erie Canal immediately generated huge amounts of new economic activity from New York City to the Great Lakes states. Some historians still regard it as the single most important public works project in American history.

In 1817 De Witt Clinton was elected governor of the state of New York. He served three terms as governor, but his third term was cut short when he died on February 11, 1828, in the state capital of Albany.

Lakes timber, minerals, and crops soared. The holds of westbound ships, meanwhile, were crammed with factory-made textiles and farming tools intended for the immigrant families that were pouring into the newly accessible farmlands of the upper Midwest. Many of these changes were evident within a few months of the canal's opening. "It is an impressive sight to gaze up and down the canal" from one of the numerous bridges that spanned the Erie, declared one admirer. "In either direction, as far as the eye can see, long lines of boats can be observed. By night, their flickering head lamps give the impression of swarms of fireflies."[15]

This surge in economic activity from the Erie Canal also sparked explosive growth and economic development in Great Lakes cities such as Cleveland, Buffalo, and Detroit that had been frontier outposts only a few years earlier. In 1820, for example, only two thousand people lived in Buffalo. Ten years after the canal opened, though, the city's population stood at more than twenty thousand residents, most of whom supported themselves in some aspect of the shipping trade.

The stunning success of the Erie Canal convinced investors, engineers, and lawmakers all across the country to launch canal-building schemes of their own. None of these systems matched the Erie Canal in size and impact, but many of them had significant regional economic benefit. By 1850 more than 3,700 miles (5,955km) of canals laced the American interior. Finally, the example of the Erie Canal prompted investment in other public works projects that further fueled America's incredible economic expansion. In the 1850s, for example, the completion of the massive Sault Ste. Marie Canals (also known as the Soo Locks) on the St. Marys River between Lake Huron and Lake Superior opened the entire Superior region up for large-scale settlement, development, and commerce.

The Age of the Steamboat

The expansion of America's system of navigable waterways took place at the same time that the steam-powered engine was revolutionizing the form and function of the vessels that traveled those rivers, canals, and coastal waters. American inventor John Fitch had carried out the first successful experiments with a steam-powered boat in the 1780s and 1790s, but it was not until 1807 that the concept of steam-powered boats and

After Robert Fulton's steamboat voyage on the North River Steamboat *in 1807, shipbuilders rushed to build steamboats to carry freight up and down the nation's rivers. Here, the* Union Steamboat *travels the Saguenay River of Quebec in 1880.*

Robert Fulton, Father of the Steamboat

Steamboating icon Robert Fulton ranks as one of the most legendary figures in American business history. He did not actually invent the steamboat, as is commonly believed, but he proved that it could be effectively used for moneymaking purposes. In addition, Fulton's fleet of New York City–based steamers made his business enterprise one of the first major transportation-based corporations in the United States.

Fulton was born on November 14, 1765, in Lancaster County, Pennsylvania. As a young man he briefly pursued a career as a painter, but by the early 1790s most of his attention was focused on industrial and mechanical engineering. He first devoted his energies to canal building and experimental submarine designs. In 1802 he formed a business partnership with Robert Livingston (1746–1813), an American diplomat who held an exclusive right to operate steam-driven boats in New York State for a twenty-year period.

Bankrolled by Livingston, Fulton experimented with improvements of steamboat designs first created by fellow American John Fitch. In 1807 he unveiled a steam-powered boat called the *North River Steamboat*. This vessel was a great commercial success, and it ushered in the age of the steamboat across America. Fulton spent the next several years designing new steamboats, building steam engines at an engine works in New Jersey, and amassing a fortune from his partnership with Livingston. He died on February 24, 1815.

ships really caught the attention of the American public. That year, on August 18, entrepreneur Robert Fulton took the *North River Steamboat* (not the *Clermont*, as many textbooks erroneously state) 150 miles (241km) up the Hudson River from New York, then took a ship full of paying passengers back down to the city.

Fulton's steamboat voyage caused a stir up and down the eastern seaboard of the United States. Shipbuilders rushed to build steamboats that could be used to carry freight up and down the nation's rivers. As these vessels joined the nation's bustling water transport system, farmers and factory owners alike marveled at the speed with which the steamboats could deliver goods to distant markets. The intense competition between steamer companies, meanwhile, kept freight charges low for both producers and consumers.

Another key milestone in the development of the steamboat—described by one scholar as "the first great American contribution to modern technology"[16]—was the development of a high-pressure steam engine. Fulton and other early steamboat innovators had powered their boats with Watt steam engines. But these engines were not strong enough to power boats along large rivers with strong currents. Steamboats became much more powerful and efficient after

Pennsylvania inventor Oliver Evans and Richard Trevithick of Wales—working independently of one another—developed a high-pressure steam engine in the opening years of the nineteenth century. "The Watt engine, which had helped to spark the Industrial Revolution and was the most fundamentally important technological development since the printing press three hundred years earlier, was obsolete after only three decades," observed one scholar. "The pace of change had already begun the relentless acceleration that continues to this day."[17]

Before long it was clear that a transportation revolution was taking place in America. As one Cincinnati resident stated in 1828, "the steam engine in five years has enabled us to anticipate a state of things, which in the ordinary course of events, it would have required a century to produce."[18] The new high-pressure steam engines established, once and for all, that the country's mighty rivers were no longer one-way highways. Steam power now gave steamboats the ability to go upstream even against the powerful river currents of the Mississippi, the Missouri, and the Ohio rivers. As a result, these and other waterways gained more economic importance than ever before. The Missisippi River system, for example, "provided no less than sixteen thousand miles of navigable waters that drained an area of more than a million square miles from western New York State to Montana," noted one historian. "Much of it was the finest agricultural land on earth with almost limitless economic potential. Much of it was also rich in minerals."[19] Steam power unlocked all of these riches.

Steady Growth in Manufacturing

Advances in steam technology took place against the backdrop of slow but steady growth in factory operations in the United States in the first three decades of the nineteenth century. Most of this early industrialization continued to take place in New England. It was here that Oliver Evans—the same man who designed the influential high-pressure steam engine— developed fully automated flour mill operations in the 1790s. As one scholar noted, "Until Oliver Evans, no one had conceived of the factory itself as a machine, yet Evans' flour mill was exactly that: You poured grain in one end, and flour came out the other. Except for adjusting, maintaining, and monitoring, the process needed no human labor whatever."[20]

New England was also the region where America's first great industry, textile manufacturing, was centered. In 1830 those textile factories still dominated the landscape of U.S. industry. A partial survey of U.S. industry in 1832, for example, revealed that thirty-one of the thirty-six factories in America that had more than 250 employees were textile mills. As time passed, however, this situation gradually changed.

From 1820 to 1840 alone, capital investment in manufacturing facilities in the United States jumped from $50 million to more than $250 million. Some of this early investment came from British business interests, but overall the surge in investment was a domestic phenomenon. American lawmakers in local, state, and federal governments provided all sorts of economic aid to industrializing businesses, including tax exemptions and special arrangements to limit competition.

State governments were particularly energetic in funding and incorporating new businesses and other public "improvements." Between 1816 and 1826, for example, legislators in Ohio incorporated eighteen turnpikes, seven bridges, two harbors, seven banks, one insurance company, one waterworks, one woolen mill, one ironmaking factory, one mining company, five colleges and a seminary, eleven academies, six school and literary societies, eight libraries, and nine charitable, religious, and historical societies.[21] Banks also first emerged as a major investing force in American business during this era. Some of this investment capital went into textiles, of course, but a lot of it was funneled into new industries such as steam shipping, railroads, and various manufacturing niches.

These factors contributed to a decade of tremendous manufacturing expansion in the 1840s. Factories that produced all sorts of goods—some intended for household use, others for use in various business operations—proliferated all across the eastern half of the United States. And some modest factories even began to appear in the American West, where the steamboat had opened new opportunities for farmers and mining interests. "The steamboat appeared as an angel of deliverance [for western com-

Oliver Evans developed the first automated factory that needed only minor human intervention to ensure that the process was maintained.

munities]," writes one historian. "Steam did not wholly banish muscle power from the western rivers. But it reawakened visions of accelerating development and gave new reign to prophecies of western greatness."[22]

By the early 1850s American factories were producing so many innovative and useful products in such great volumes that England—the original home of the industrial revolution—approved formal studies of the "American system of manufacturing." These reports marveled at the speed with which small U.S. shops and mills were expanding into major employers. They also reported admiringly about the enormous volume of economic activity that was taking place in America. But they also admitted that it would be difficult for England to duplicate such success, for the United States simply had more people and natural resources to draw on.

Coal—The Fuel of Industrialization

One of the most important natural resources that drove America's rapid industrialization was coal. The steam engines that powered America's factories and steamships needed fuel, and as the nineteenth century progressed, coal increasingly replaced wood as the fuel of choice. It also became the main heating fuel for households across much of America.

The first great center of coal production was Pennyslvania, which held massive deposits of both high-quality anthracite coal and lower quality bituminous coal. During the 1820s coal mining activity transformed Pittsburgh from a small village into a bustling city full of glassmakers and ironworks—both fuel-intensive industries that were heavily dependent on coal. In addition, by 1845 more than 2 million tons (1.8 million t) of anthracite had been transported out of the hills of western Pennsylvania via steamboat and

Miners load coal onto a conveyor at a Pennsylvania mine in 1918. By mid-century, western Pennsylvania produced more coal than the rest of the country combined.

railroad to factories and households of the eastern cities. In fact, western Pennsylvania produced more anthracite coal than the rest of the country combined at mid century, and it employed more than two-thirds of the industry's workforce until the 1860s.[23]

Anthracite coal also was pivotal in the development of the railroad industry. First of all, it ranked as a major source of revenue for virtually all mid-century railroad companies as their trains delivered the coal around the country. But its importance to the iron industry also made it an important element in the overall buildup of the railroad industry's infrastructure. During the 1830s and 1840s, innovative processes of smelting iron from anthracite coal enabled American iron makers to dramatically expand production of high-quality, reasonably priced iron rails and other materials that were essential to the railroads. Not surprisingly, then, several leading railroad companies of this era also became major players in the coal industry. "Anthracite country is often called the cradle of American railroading, and with good reason," summarizes one historian.

> The anthracite mine operators were the first Americans to use rails, and they greatly advanced the science of building railways. . . . The Philadelphia and Reading Railroad, one of the nation's largest and most powerful companies, dominated the area, but there would be five railways so intermingled with the anthracite trade that coal and rail-

roading were often considered a single industry.[24]

A Revolution in Iron Making

Ironically, these industrial advances might have happened even sooner but for the fact that American iron makers—unlike virtually all other industrial sectors—were slow to embrace certain technological innovations. In the 1820s British iron makers had introduced the coal-fired blast furnace. These coal-fired forges generated higher temperatures than charcoal, an inferior but plentiful fuel that had long been used in the industry. The higher temperatures generated enabled ironmasters to burn off a greater percentage of carbon and thus produce iron products of superior strength and durability.

Within a matter of a few years, Great Britain's iron industry had used this technology to vault to the forefront of the world's iron makers. In fact, the country became an exporter of iron after years of being an importer. In the United States, though, furnace and forge owners stubbornly maintained their allegiance to the old charcoal-based production system that the British had abandoned.

The American iron industry was slow to follow the British example for two reasons. First, the U.S. government had attached heavy tariffs on iron imports from England. These taxes made American iron less expensive to purchase than English iron. In addition, the demand for iron goods was so extraordinarily high across

Ironworkers stand in front of the Ensley blast furnace near Birmingham, Alabama, in 1890. Originally, the American iron industry lagged behind the British by clinging to a charcoal-based production system.

the country that American forge owners did not have to worry about producing works of premium quality on a timely basis. They knew that virtually everything they produced, from firearms to stoves to parts for ships and locomotives, would be snapped up as soon as it appeared on the marketplace.

In the 1830s, though, some U.S. iron makers finally began to invest in the blast-furnace technology that had been such a boon to the British. Forge owners who made the switch from charcoal to coal were enormously successful. Their increased output was mostly responsible for a doubling of U.S. iron production during the 1840s. The changing competitive environment also forced some of the smaller and less efficient iron

makers out of business. Large corporations with impressive arrays of forges and rolling mills assumed greater prominence than ever before. These corporations entered the 1850s in good shape to meet the looming business challenges and opportunities associated with the impending opening of the West to settlement and development.

The Mechanization of Farming

As the first half of the nineteenth century drew to a close, industrialization was even transforming the lives—and livelihoods—of rural American farmers who lived miles away from the bustling factories, railroad yards, and crowded immigrant neighborhoods of the cities.

America had been a nation of farmers since the colonial era, and agriculture remained the leading area of economic activity in the United States well into the Age of Industrialization. Some farming families viewed the sweeping economic and social changes ushered in by the industrial revolution with greater fear and skepticism than their urban countrymen. But many others seized the new economic opportunities that came with industrialization, such as increased access via railroads and steamships to markets that lay hundreds or even thousands of miles away. And America's farmers never would have been able to provide for the needs of the rapidly growing population of the United States—or meet the growing demand for cotton and other crops overseas—if they had not embraced some elements of industrialization in their own operations.

Eli Whitney began the mechanization of farming with the invention of the cotton gin in the 1790s.

The first major technological innovation that shaped American agriculture was Eli Whitney's cotton gin. This revolutionary tool, first unveiled in the 1790s, made cotton production a much more efficient and profitable enterprise than it had ever been before. It single-handedly turned the economy of the American South into one that was overwhelmingly dependent on "King Cotton." Unfortunately, the stunning growth in demand for cotton—a labor-intensive crop—made white southern commerce and culture more dependent on slavery than ever before. This state of affairs put the South at loggerheads with the North, which developed a thriving industrial economy and strong moral qualms about slavery during the first half of the nineteenth century. The two regions proved unable to bridge their differences, and in 1861 their long-simmering feud finally exploded into the American Civil War.

Cyrus McCormick and the Wheat Boom

Inventor Cyrus McCormick was born in Virginia on February 15, 1809. He spent his youth working on his father's twelve-hundred-acre grain and livestock farm (485.6ha). The long hours he spent cutting wheat by hand made an enormous impression on him. In 1831 the twenty-two-year-old invented a mechanical reaping machine that could harvest wheat far more swiftly and efficiently than could be accomplished by manual labor.

McCormick struggled to sell his invention for the next several years. By the mid-1840s, though, American wheat growers were so eager to increase their yields and streamline their operations that they began to buy McCormick's reaper in large numbers. McCormick kept up with the rising demand by establishing a factory in Chicago that mass-produced the reapers. The distribution of these reapers across America's heartland has been frequently cited as a major factor in the surge in American wheat production that occurred in the 1850s and subsequent decades.

By the mid-1850s McCormick was a millionaire. He invested heavily in Chicago real estate and U.S. railroads, and he expanded his reaper sales into Europe. After his death in 1884, his son Cyrus Jr. took over the business. In 1902 the company merged with four other makers of agricultural machine products to create a giant firm called International Harvester. This company remained one of the largest agricultural equipment companies in the world throughout the twentieth century.

A worker drives a horse-drawn McCormick harvester while harvesting wheat in 1916.

Other technological advances in the field of agriculture had fewer controversial side effects than the cotton gin. In fact, most of them were welcomed by all Americans with open arms, for they made the tasks of raising and harvesting crops much less laborious and time-consuming than they had been for previous generations. Agricultural machinery such as William Pennock's 1841 grain drill and John Deere's 1837 wrought iron, "singing" plow enabled farmers to sow seeds much more quickly than ever before, while new threshing machines introduced in the 1830s and 1840s dramatically cut harvesting time.

The single most important mechanical tool to appear on American farms in the first half of the nineteenth century, though, was Cyrus McCormick's mechanical reaper. McCormick's invention, which he first displayed in 1831, mechanized every component of the wheat harvesting process, and it freed farmers and hired hands from the slow, exhausting task of reaping wheat with handheld tools.

McCormick's machine was so large in size and revolutionary in its capabilities that at first American farmers flatly refused even to try the machine. They assumed it could not work as well as McCormick promised. The inventor failed to sell a single reaper for more than a decade, and in the early 1840s he was still selling only a handful of machines each year. In 1845, though, McCormick's fortunes changed when poor weather produced grain crop failures across Great Britain. British authorities responded to the disaster by removing several laws that had prevented American farmers from selling wheat in Great Britain. As American wheat growers scrambled to meet the soaring demand for their product, they finally turned to McCormick, who had built a factory in Chicago for the mass production of his harvesters. Within a decade, McCormick harvesters were rumbling across American farms from Ohio to the western edge of the Great Plains. "With McCormick's reaper, one man could harvest eight acres a day, not one, and the American Middle West could become the bread basket of the world," writes one historian.

The McCormick reaper not only greatly enlarged the potential size of American grain crops, it changed how Americans have earned their livelihoods. With the introduction of the reaper and the endless parade of mechanical agricultural equipment that followed, the percentage of American workers engaged in agriculture has steadily declined, even while agricultural output has continued to grow. The McCormick reaper thus helped crucially to supply the labor needed in the great expansion of American industry that followed the Civil War.[25]

Chapter Three

The "Iron Horse," the Telegraph, and Westward Expansion

In the second half of the nineteenth century, the American industrial revolution entered its golden age. This was an era in which new industrial marvels, economic growth, and territorial expansion all seemed to be marching along together, carrying the United States to new heights of wealth, opportunity, and power. The steam-powered railroad, which ranks as perhaps the single most important invention of the nineteenth century, was an essential force in this growth. But many other vitally important inventions and innovations also occurred during this era, from the telegraph to the mass production of steel. By the end of the nineteenth century, these interdependent industries had made the United States a global economic power—and ushered in the age of the modern corporation.

The Arrival of the Railroad

The first railroads that were advanced enough to be used for profitable commercial activity appeared in the late 1820s and early 1830s. England's first practical railroad was George Stephenson's Liverpool and Manchester Railway, which began operating in 1830. Nearly simultaneously, the Baltimore and Ohio (B&O) Railroad established itself as the first successful steam-powered railroad company in the United States. Neither of these railroads—or the ones that soon followed—were based on the work or invention of a single individual. Rather, they were based on the collective efforts of numerous engineers and inventors who mastered various components of railroad design and operation.

Unlike canals, rivers, and rough roadways, railroads could be built nearly anywhere, and they could operate year-round in all kinds of weather. These characteristics not only made the railroad a wonderful resource for transporting freight from one place to another, but it also gave travelers a speedy and comfortable transportation alternative. These advantages

A train on the Baltimore and Ohio Railroad in 1858. The B&O was the first successful steam-powered railroad company in the United States.

were clear to American engineers and investors, who flocked to the new technology. In 1830 the railroad industry barely existed. One decade later, however, nearly 3,000 miles (4,828km) of track line had been laid across the United States, mostly in the East. By 1850 more than 9,000 miles (14,484km) of railroad lines snaked across America, and by the time the Civil War erupted in 1861, more than 30,000 miles (48,280km) of line had been built. Most of these lines were in the North, which gave that side a tremendous military advantage during the war.

Many of the railroad lines that were built in the 1840s and 1850s connected cities to other cities, but others were built to link mining facilities and timber tracts to factories and mills. Wherever they

were constructed, the railroads changed America's social, business, and environmental landscape in lasting ways. In some respects their legacy was a positive one, but in other respects they had a dark side. For example, railroads gave rural farmers, ranchers, and mining companies access to markets they had never had before, but they also crushed numerous steamboat operations that had been raking in enormous profits in the pre–railroad era. Cities and towns blossomed along rail lines, which pulsed with economic activity. But this fact gave railroad owners excessive power over the future of entire communities. "It became a matter of a railroad's choice whether a town was to become a metropolis, a tank-town whistle stop—or a ghost town," writes one historian. "The town or valley or trading post on the prairie through which a railroad passed knew it had a future, but the place without a railroad was headed for oblivion."[26]

The railroad also went a long way toward making the ever-growing United States feel like a single nation rather than a vast collection of remote communities. But in many regions of the country, the forces it unleashed had a destructive impact on the American environment. Entire forests were carried away on the backs of railroads. In addition, towns and cities nurtured by the railroads turned their surrounding countrysides into wheat fields, grazing lands, and industrial sites. Alto-

gether, these swift economic and cultural changes prompted one visitor to America, English writer William Makepeace Thackeray, to comment that "we who have lived before the railways were made belong to another world."[27]

Finally, railroads were the first U.S. industry to introduce modern management principles to their operations. By mid century, railroad companies had become so large and had established offices over such vast geographical areas that they were forced to adopt organizational structures with clear lines of authority and responsibility. These operational structures, which were led by large numbers of

Workers laying track on the Nevada section of Central Pacific Railroad in 1868. The railroad was an essential part of the expansion of settlers into the West.

salaried officers and managers, eventually filtered into the steel industry and other major industries that emerged in the late nineteenth century.

Westward Expansion and the "Iron Horse"

The railroad also ranked as a vital instrument of western settlement. During the first half of the nineteenth century, the United States had used the Louisiana Purchase of 1803, the treaty terms of the Mexican-American War (1846–1848), and other actions to expand its territory from the eastern banks of the Mississippi River all the way to the Pacific Ocean. Most Americans were convinced that it was God's will that they tame this vast wilderness, defeat (or destroy) its Native American inhabitants, and use the region's natural resources for the betterment of themselves and the larger nation. This belief that Americans were destined to conquer and settle the West became known as Manifest Destiny.

White settlers flooded into the West during the second half of the nineteenth century. Eager to make better lives for themselves and their families, these pioneers took advantage of cheap land grants and other government programs designed to encourage settlement of the West. They established farms, mining operations, towns, and cities in places that had been Indian hunting grounds only a few years earlier. By the close of the nineteenth century the vast lands that lay between the Pacific Ocean and the Mississippi River supported cities and industries that rivaled all but the greatest metropolises of the East. "For all the men who were broken and women who were dried to leather by the frontier, for all the slaughter and waste of resources, for all the unrealized dreams, the promise of the West was nevertheless fulfilled,"[28] asserted one review of the era.

The transformation of the West would never have been possible, though, without the "iron horse," as the railroad was often called in western communities. The rapid development of this transportation option had transformed the economy and culture of the eastern United States in the 1830s and 1840s, and it did the same thing in the West in the second half of the century. Vast networks of railroad lines moved settlers from the East to the West, gave manufacturers and farmers the means to send their products greater distances than ever before, and greatly increased the speed by which everything from iron ore to information could be delivered cross-country. "Lumber, coal, glass, iron, construction, and lubrication businesses located anywhere near the new [rail] lines prospered in their wake," affirms one historian. "Bankers, brokers, printers, newspaper editors, whalers, even sandwich-makers, cashed in on the new riches. Railways equally benefited shippers, importers and exporters, manufacturers, miners, farmers, and almost every other occupational group imaginable."[29]

In many cases, railroad companies took an even more active role in distributing western lands than state, territorial, or federal authorities. In 1850, for example, the federal government authorized the distribution of more than 3.7 million acres (1.5 million ha) of public land to railroad companies in Alabama, Mississippi, and Illinois. Specifically, these grants provided beneficiaries in the railroad industry with a 200-foot right-of-way corridor (61m) and alternating parcels of land on either side of the corridor, which they were free to develop or sell off to settlers as they saw fit.

These and other grant programs were essential in the settlement and development of the Great Lakes region at mid century, but they were even more important in spurring settlement in the West. Congress and various state and territorial governments granted Western railroads a total of about 116 million acres (47 million ha) in land grants. Four railroads—the Northern Pacific, the Atchison, Topeka & Santa Fe, the Union Pacific, and the Southern Pacific—received over 70 percent of the total land awarded. These allocations of public land gave the railroads a huge economic incentive to tame the West. "The main objective [of railroads] was to build up settlement as a means of generating freight to carry," explains one scholar. "Railroad companies, especially those possessing land grants, were colonizers of the Great Plains on a big scale. They carried forward on a vast scale the work that had been done on a lesser scale by colonizing companies on the seaboard in the colonial period."[30]

Over time, the railroads became so closely associated with the health and vitality of the growing American empire that many people used the language of mythology to describe the trains roaring across the countryside. Asa Whitney, who helped build the nation's first transcontinental railroad in the 1860s, declared that when traveling by train, "time & space are annihilated by steam, we pass through a City a town, yea a country, like an arrow from Jupiters Bow."[31] A writer in an 1853 issue of *Putnam's Monthly Magazine* described the American train as

the earthshaker, the fire-breather, which tramples down the hills, which outruns the laggard winds, which leaps over the rivers, which grinds the rocks to powder and breaks down the gates of the mountains. . . . Shall not cities be formed from his vaporous breath, and men spring up from the cinders of his furnace? Imagine then, the Vulcan-wrought engine rushing from sea to sea, dispensing lightning from its sides and thunder from its wheels— the one-eyed smiths from the doors of their workshops in the mountain, watching the progress of the prodigy with grim delight![32]

New Heights of Industrialization

As new railroad arteries sprouted across the American landscape and more land was converted to agricultural use, the United States experienced a massive increase in its levels of crop production. From 1870 to 1900 the total number of American farms more than doubled. The

The Homestead Act

Of all the land distribution programs that were instituted to encourage Western settlement in the nineteenth century, none was as important as the Homestead Act of 1862. This act was specifically created to lure settlers to territory opened as a result of the passage of the 1854 Kansas-Nebraska Act. According to the terms of this act, any American citizen or immigrant alien who was white, male, and twenty-one years old or the head of a family could take possession of 160 acres of unsettled public land by paying a ten-dollar claim fee. After five years of residence and "improvement" of the parcel, he would then receive final title at no additional cost. Later amendments to the act increased the size of the grant to 640 acres and shortened the necessary period of residence.

The Homestead Act enabled millions of American settlers to successfully establish themselves in the West. But the inexpensive terms of the Act hid the true cost of pursuing a new life in the Western states and territories. Much of the land that was available through the Act was of only marginal quality for raising crops or livestock, because timber and mining companies and wealthy cattle ranchers were able to use their political connections to snap up the best land. In addition, many poor farmers were at the mercy of forces beyond their control, such as weather and railroad freight rates.

A family of homesteaders poses with their wagon in Loup Valley, Nebraska, while on their way to claim their share of government land in 1886.

In this 1882 cartoon, American industrialists Cornelius Vanderbilt, Jay Gould, Russell Sage, and Cyrus W. Field divide the United States into a railroad monopoly among themselves as Europe looks on.

total amount of land set aside for farming also expanded dramatically during these three decades, from a little over 400 million acres (162 million ha) to more than 840 million acres (340 million ha).

Not surprisingly, this expansion in land under cultivation and the arrival of mechanized farming—as well as more sophisticated use of fertilization and irrigation techniques—generated huge jumps in crop production. Wheat production jumped from 250 million to 600 million bushels (6.8 million t to 16.3 million t) from 1870 to 1900, and corn production rose from 1.1 million to 2.7 million bushels (.03 million t to .07 million t). Cotton production in the post–Civil War era surged as well. As the Reconstruction era gave way to discriminatory Jim Crow laws across the Deep South, white planters reasserted their power over poor white and black sharecroppers. By the close of the nineteenth century, these economically destitute and politically powerless sharecroppers were helping to produce more than 10 million bales a year for the southern cotton lords.

Investment capital and settlement patterns also established manufacturing in towns and cities that had been little more than trading posts a few decades earlier. Many textile operations gradually drifted out of New England to the South, where the costs of hiring workers and shipping cotton were much lower. Meanwhile, factories and mills followed the millions of settlers who had been attracted to the West by reports of gold strikes, promises of good farmland, or steady work in timber and mining camps. As one historian summarized:

> Industrialization produced towns and cities, in some of the most difficult conditions imaginable, in the mountains of Colorado or on the plains of eastern Montana, as westerners sought the amenities of urban life. Schools, churches, and opera houses quickly followed the railroad station, bank, and general mercantile store. If there was a unique element in the American West, it was the speed of this transformation.[33]

All of this economic activity and political influence turned the nation's leading railroad owners, financiers, and mining executives into fabulously wealthy and powerful men. Some of these men, such as Jay Gould, Cornelius Vanderbilt, John D. Rockefeller, and J.P. Morgan, became household names in America. But fame did not necessarily translate into respect among the wider American public. In fact, railroad magnates and other industrial tycoons of the late nineteenth century became widely known as "robber barons" —a negative term that reflected the common belief that these men built their fortunes through ruthless exploitation of workers, cunning manipulation of lawmakers and officials, and savage attacks on competitors.

Fuel for the Fires of Industry

The robber barons were aware of their controversial reputation, but they paid little attention. Instead, they maintained their focus on advancing American industrialization and increasing the riches that could be gained from it. To this end, one of their highest priorities was finding new energy resources to feed the factories, foundries, and railroads of the industrial revolution. Over the course of the nineteenth century, two substances— coal and oil—emerged as the precious fuels of the Industrial Age.

In colonial America and for much of the pre–Civil War era, most of the nation's energy needs had been met with wood. Railroad locomotives and household stoves alike were fueled in this manner. Most Americans were ignorant not only of coal's superior qualities as a source of heat and energy, but also of the vast ribbons of coal that existed in the hills of Pennsylvania and other parts of the country.

The appetite for firewood was so great, in fact, that its impact on Ameri-

A Scoundrel Among the Robber Barons

Even among the corporate giants and financiers that the American public angrily dubbed "robber barons," the industrialist Jayson "Jay" Gould had a dark reputation. Born in Roxbury, New York, on May 27, 1836, Gould left the family farm as a youth to work as a surveyor, clerk, and blacksmith. In the early 1860s he moved to New York City and became active in the stock market. Within a few years, he manipulated stock in small railroads and other companies so effectively that he became a wealthy man.

Ambitious and competitive, Gould dove deeper into the worlds of stocks and railroads. In the late 1860s and 1870s he orchestrated a series of shady business deals, including a bold scheme to corner the gold market in 1869. This particular plan backfired when Gould's maneuvering triggered a panic on Wall Street that sent all stocks—including ones that Gould owned—plummeting. But other stock manipulation schemes enabled him to recover his losses and add to his fortune within a few years.

In the 1870s Gould concentrated on building up his railroad investments. By 1881 he controlled a railroad empire that included profitable lines from Boston to Omaha, and his warlike attitude toward competing railways was known far and wide. He also seized a controlling stake in Western Union, the greatest of the telegraph companies that emerged in the post–Civil War era. In these and many other business dealings, he became notorious as a ruthless double-crosser who tried to squeeze every last cent of profit out of every man he employed.

By the time Gould died on December 2, 1892, he was universally regarded as one of the most hated men in America. As biographer Maury Klein wrote, "two generations of operators, businessmen, bankers, lawyers, coupon clippers, stockholders, politicians, reformers, journalists, ministers, and other guardians of the public morals reviled him as the supreme villain of his age."

Source: Maury Klein, *The Life and Legend of Jay Gould*. Baltimore: Johns Hopkins University Press, 1986.

can forests was far greater than timber cutting for lumber. From 1811 to 1867, fuel cutters converted an estimated 200,000 square miles (518,000 sq. km) of forest into firewood.[34] This incredible rate of deforestation alarmed some Americans, who urged their citizens to take better care of the wilderness. But most Americans ignored such warnings because they believed that the supply of land and resources within the nation's borders was inexhaustible.

After the Civil War, though, coal consumption steadily increased. The inexpensive mineral was ideally suited for use in industrial forges, and it also became the preferred energy source in many households. In the mid-1880s coal finally surpassed wood as the nation's leading energy source, and by the close of the nineteenth century, coal accounted for nearly three-quarters of the nation's total energy use. Virtually all of this coal came from domestic sources, as mining companies tapped into vast deposits in Pennsylvania, West Virginia, and Ohio, as well as Colorado and other western states.

By the beginning of the twentieth century, Americans from Maine to California recognized that the nation's economic future was heavily dependent on "King Coal." Coal's main rival as a source of America's energy needs was oil. In the 1840s the oil industry barely existed. But American engineers developed new ways of accessing oil in the 1850s, and inventors quickly figured out new uses for the substance. A by-product of oil called kerosene replaced whale oil as the nation's main fuel for lanterns by the 1870s, and oil refineries also developed forms of gasoline that were used as fuel oils, solvents, and lubricants. In the 1880s and 1890s the oil industry emerged as a major economic force in the United States. This emergence was partly due to steadily escalating demand for oil and partly due to the consolidation of the oil industry in the hands of one brilliant and ruthless entrepreneur, John D. Rockefeller.

Two Pacific Northwest loggers stand next to felled Douglas fir trees. Until the late 1860s firewood was the main source of energy for the United States.

Rockefeller had entered the oil business in the early 1860s as a minor investor. By the end of the 1880s, though, Rockefeller had built his Standard Oil Company into a financial empire without equal in the United States. It was the dominant producer, refiner, and seller of oil across the country. By the close of the nineteenth century, wrote Rockefeller biographer Ron Chernow,

Standard Oil seemed omnipotent. Everything about its operation was colossal: 20,000 wells poured their output into 4,000 miles of Standard Oil pipelines, carrying the crude to seaboard or to 5,000 Standard Oil tank cars. The [combined companies] now employed 100,000 people and superintended the export of 50,000 barrels of oil daily. Rockefeller's creation could be discussed only in superlatives: It was the biggest and richest, the most feared and admired business organization in the world.[35]

The Era of Steel

America's switch to coal and oil was of enormous benefit to the nation's iron industry, which used a flurry of innovations to transform itself into a maker of steel in the 1860s and 1870s. Prior to the Civil War, the United States produced less than 12,000 tons (10,886t) of steel annually. Steelmaking was expensive and time consuming, so the substance was generally reserved for special products such as prairie plows and fine-edged tools.

In the 1860s, though, the Bessemer steelmaking process was introduced in iron foundries in England and the United States. This technological advance was named after Sir Henry Bessemer of England, but an American ironmaster named William Kelly actually made the same breakthrough at about the same time. Both men discovered a method of creating steel by using air to remove excess carbon and other impurities in molten pig iron. Armed with this innovation, iron foundries were able to process steel in far greater volumes than ever before.

Steel was a far stronger product than iron, so when steel production became commercially viable, the impact was felt across the entire U.S. economy. Steel became the material of choice for everything from railroad lines to the skyscrapers that sprouted along the skyline of numerous cities. By 1880 annual American steel production reached an incredible 1.2 million tons (1.1 million t)—one hundred times more than the industry was producing a mere twenty years earlier. During this time the industry also became one of the country's leading employers of Irish, German, Russian, Italian, Polish, and English immigrants. As one historian noted, "A vast pool of unskilled labor lay only an ocean away [and] the steel mills of America soon exerted a strong gravitational pull on the European masses."[36]

A great many of these European immigrants went to work for Andrew Carnegie. The Carnegie Steel Company, which was masterminded by Carnegie and his partner Henry Clay Frick, had

Pittsburgh steel workers use a Bessemer converter to form steel in 1895. The invention of the Bessemer process allowed steel to be produced in much great quantities and, as a result, it became the building material of choice.

been carefully constructed in the 1870s and 1880s so that it had a presence in every aspect of the steel industry. Carnegie's personal secretary, James Howard Bridge, recalls that by the early 1890s the Carnegie steel empire

> owned its own mines, dug its ore with machines of amazing power, loaded it into its own steamers, landed it at its own ports, transported

it on its own railroads, distributed it among its many blast furnaces, and smelted it with coke similarly brought from its own coal mines and ovens, and with limestone brought from its own quarries. From the moments these crude stuffs were dug out of the earth until they flowed in a stream of liquid steel into the ladles, there was never a price, profit, or royalty paid to an outsider.[37]

By the close of the nineteenth century, Carnegie Steel was not only America's leading steelmaker, it was also producing more steel than the entire British steel industry.

An Age of Economic Interdependence

The rise of Carnegie Steel and the rest of the U.S. steel industry could never have occurred, however, without coal's emergence as a foundry fuel. Nor could the steel industry have risen to the heights that it did if America's railroads had not developed such an enormous appetite for steel rails. These realities underscore the fact that America's entire industrial revolution was based on various industries working together. The steel industry, for example, had an enormous influence on the real estate industry, for it provided developers and builders with the necessary raw material to construct the railroad depots, dams, harbors, bridges, factories, and office buildings that became the foundations of modern American cities. Similarly, western cattle ranching became much more lucrative after the 1870s, when refrigerated railcars made it much easier to deliver beef to market. In addition, historian John Steele Gordon noted that the needs of the railroad industry sustained a wide array of manufacturers:

Railroads required enormous quantities of industrial goods: locomotives, freight and passenger cars, rails, cross ties, spikes, and bridge members, to name just a few. At first, nearly all these had to be imported from England. But as the American demand for these commodities grew, more and more American entrepreneurs began to supply them, driving the industrial revolution in this country more than any other single force.[38]

Perhaps no industry benefited more from the railroads than the telegraph industry. American inventor Samuel Morse had unveiled the telegraph in the mid-1830s, and by the early 1850s telegraph wires were being strung up across America with feverish excitement. "It is hard to imagine today, when satellites and undersea cables keep every part of the globe in instant communication with every other part, just how slowly news spread [before the arrival of the telegraph]," explains one historian.

The battles of Lexington and Concord, the opening events of the American Revolution, occurred on Wednesday, April 19, 1775. But news of the events reached New York only on Sunday, April 23, and Philadelphia on April 24. . . . And it was on May 28, fully five and a half weeks later, that the British cabinet in London learned, to its horror, that the long-smoldering crisis in America had flashed into open war.[39]

The telegraph system gave Americans (and people around the world) the power to communicate instantaneously with people hundreds or even thousands of miles away. The first telegraph lines were strung

Samuel Morse, Inventor of the Telegraph

Samuel Finley Breese Morse was born on April 27, 1791, in Charlestown, Massachusetts. The son of a minister, he attended Yale and spent several years studying painting in England. Morse eventually established a thriving portrait studio in Boston. But in the early 1830s he became fascinated with early experiments with electromagnetism, which some scientists believed could be harnessed to send messages long distances over wire.

Morse teamed with Alfred Vail to build a telegraph prototype that could transmit electrical pulses of varying length—an alphabet of dots and dashes that came to be known as Morse code—over electrical wires to stations hundreds or even thousands of miles away from one another. Morse received a patent for his telegraph invention in 1837, and in 1843 he received a long-sought grant from the U.S. Congress to build

a telegraph line between Washington, D.C., and Baltimore, Maryland. Several months later, on May 24, 1844, Morse successfully transmitted a message between the Washington and Baltimore stations. Word of this triumph triggered a frenzy of telegraph network building up and down the East Coast.

During the second half of the nineteenth century, Morse's invention spread all across the United States and changed American life forever. It also made the inventor a wealthy man. In his later years Morse divided his time between charitable efforts, political activism, and his large family. He died in New York City on April 2, 1872.

Samuel Morse poses beside his invention of the telegraph.

up between eastern cities. By the 1860s, though, they were following railroad lines out into the western frontier, to the great mutual benefit of both industries. Telegraph companies used existing railroad corridors to erect thousands of miles of telegraph wire at a fraction of the cost that would have been involved if they had had to clear land themselves. In return, railroad companies were able to use telegraphs to dispatch trains, adjust business schedules, and modernize western mining towns and farm communities that provided freight for the railroads.

These sorts of strategic alliances across industries became so commonplace during the Age of Industrialization that they became a standard feature of American business. Savvy and resourceful entrepreneurs and executives used such alliances to build enormous corporations and trusts that wielded great control over the marketplace. By the close of the nineteenth century, however, these corporate giants wielded so much power—and used it so ruthlessly against the workers that toiled in their factories, shipyards, and quarries—that the American public rebelled. And as the twentieth century began, this rebellion brought major changes to the still-evolving industrial revolution.

Chapter Four

The Economic and Social Impact of the Industrial Revolution

The industrial revolution transformed virtually every aspect of American existence. Nineteenth-century technological innovations (such as the railroad and telegraph) and economic developments (such as the rise of the factory system and the corporation) provided the foundations for modern life as we know it today. Some of the social changes that accompanied industrialization were negative, for example, soaring rates of urban poverty and rising tensions between employers and workers. But the Age of Industrialization also encouraged a sustained wave of immigration to America, sparked support for public education, triggered positive advances in women's rights, and gave some Americans more leisure time and comfortable surroundings than ever before.

Immigrants and Industrial America

One of the keys to America's rapid industrialization and its settlement of the West was the massive, sustained influx of European immigrants to U.S. shores during the nineteenth century. This wave of immigration stemmed in part from problems in Europe, where political turmoil, lack of economic opportunity, and crop failures afflicted many regions. But European immigrants also made the long and difficult journey across the Atlantic Ocean in a mood of optimism and hope. They knew that factory jobs and inexpensive land for farming awaited them in America. To these struggling men and women, the United States represented a fresh start.

By 1860 nearly one out of three men living in the northern United States had been born in a foreign land. As the nineteenth century wore on, the flood of immigrants did not slow. Instead, the origins of European immigration merely shifted from Germany, England, and other western European nations to Italy, Poland, and other parts of eastern Europe.

Whatever their country of origin, these European immigrants—as well as smaller numbers of immigrants from other places like Mexico, China, and the West Indies—became essential to America's stunning economic growth. Many of them filled America's factories, steel mills, shipyards, coal mines, and oil fields, where they operated great industrial machines that rattled and roared around the clock. Other immigrants staked their futures on the Great Lakes region or the territories of the Great Plains, where they established farms or joined logging outfits and mining companies. Some of these immigrants and their families lived hundreds of miles from the nearest city, but they contributed to the industrial age as well. After all, it was their labor that provided the food, coal, iron ore, and other resources that kept the industrial cities humming.

The immigrants who settled in rural areas of the central United States and the Great Plains faced a host of challenges.

Crime, poverty, and disease were rampant in working-class neighborhoods, such as this one in New York City during the early 1900s.

Some of these obstacles, such as weather-related crop failures and high railroad freight charges, were present throughout the rural regions. Others were unique to certain areas. In various parts of the West, for example, settlers, miners, and ranchers entered into violent conflict with Native American tribes who were desperate to stop the white invaders from taking their lands and destroying their ways of life.

Nonetheless, many immigrant families who settled in America's cities would have gladly changed places with their rural brethren. Working-class people in New York City, Chicago, Boston, and other major cities lived in troubled surroundings. American cities of the nineteenth century grew so quickly that municipal governments were overwhelmed. Poverty, disease, and crime stalked the streets of many crowded urban neighborhoods. Millions of children were forced by economic circumstances to work next to their parents in factories and mills.

Many immigrants tried to shield themselves from some of these problems by gathering together in ethnic enclaves. In these neighborhoods, people could take comfort in their native languages and native customs. These settlement patterns, though, bred distrust and bigotry between isolated ethnic groups that often competed against each other for jobs and housing.

Labor Rights and Corporate Reform

As industrialization swept across America, immigrant and native-born workers alike expressed anger and frustration with their corporate employers. Most industries expected long hours of hard work from their unskilled and semi-skilled workers. Sixty- and seventy-hour work weeks were not uncommon, and many jobs took a significant physical toll. But workers were generally paid poorly, and they often endured hazardous working conditions. In fact, employers had no legal responsibility for injuries or deaths suffered in their factories, and few owners felt any moral obligation to keep their employees safe. From 1880 to 1900, 35,000 industrial workers were killed annually, and another 536,000 suffered injury. "By present standards, the age of America's first industrial revolution must be regarded as callous in its relative indifference to the welfare and safety of workers," summarizes one historian. "The unemployed worker was cast adrift. As a rule, there was no such thing as public relief, and private charity was either insufficient or offered only on demeaning terms. The risks of injury or death on the job were grievously high."[40]

American workers tried to change working conditions by joining together in labor unions. These unions bargained with employers on behalf of their members on a wide range of issues. They sought better wages and benefits, shorter work hours, more flexible work rules, and safer working conditions. In the post–Civil War era, some unions of skilled craftsmen did manage to negotiate significant wage and workplace improvements for their memberships. But unskilled and semiskilled workers did not have the same bargaining power.

A group of people examine the aftermath of the "Ludlow Massacre" in Ludlow, Colorado, where striking coal miners and their families were murdered by corporate detectives and the Colorado National Guard in 1914.

The Economic and Social Impact of the Industrial Revolution ■ 59

Instead, their efforts to improve their circumstances and better provide for their families were usually crushed by corporate owners who were determined to maximize their profits. Sometimes, big mining, railroad, and manufacturing companies with political influence even wielded National Guard troops or local police to break strikes and harass union leaders. The ruthless tactics of America's corporate giants made it hard for unions to make significant gains, and only one out of ten members of the American workforce held a union membership at the end of the nineteenth century.

Despite numerous disappointments, though, activists like Samuel Gompers of the American Federation of Labor (AFL), John Mitchell of the United Mine Workers (UMW), labor leader Mary "Mother" Jones, populist politician William Jennings Bryan, and Socialist Eugene Debs continued to fight for workers' rights in the late 1800s and the early 1900s. Their calls for economic and social justice were echoed by crusading

Muckraking Journalist Upton Sinclair

The famous American journalist Upton Beall Sinclair Jr. was born on September 20, 1878, in Baltimore, Maryland. He set out to make a career for himself as a writer and investigative reporter at an early age. Sinclair did not achieve fame, though, until he published *The Jungle* in 1906. This novel painted such a grim—and accurate—picture of the horrible conditions in the U.S. meatpacking industry that the American public demanded reforms in the industry. The U.S. Congress and President Theodore Roosevelt responded by passing the Pure Food and Drug Act and the Meat Inspection Act later in 1906.

The uproar over *The Jungle* established Sinclair as the most prominent of America's "muckrakers," a term used to describe a group of turn-of-the-century journalists who used their pens to expose political corruption, urban social problems, and corporate trickery from New York to San Francisco. As the years passed, Sinclair wrote dozens of novels, essays, and investigative reports. Many of these works reflected the author's commitment to social justice and his strong belief in socialism.

In the 1920s Sinclair's political activism led him to make two unsuccessful bids for Congress. In 1934 he won the Democratic nomination for California's governorship with a platform he called EPIC (End Poverty in California). He was defeated by Republican nominee Frank Merriam in the general election, however. Sinclair then returned to writing, and in 1943 he received the Pulitzer prize for his novel *Dragon's Teeth*. Sinclair died on November 25, 1968.

journalists such as Upton Sinclair, Ida Tarbell, and Jacob Riis. The stories published by these investigative reporters detailed crushing poverty in urban slums, brutal working conditions in industrial factories, and ways in which big business manipulated the nation's political, judicial, and economic systems.

By the dawn of the twentieth century, public calls for business and social reform were impossible to ignore. Many middle-class people had joined working-class critics in concluding that the wealthy industrialists who directed the country's huge corporations and trusts were hoarding economic and political power at the expense of their fellow citizens. These Americans welcomed the economic growth and vitality that industrialization had brought, but they worried that big business bore a heavy responsibility for the poverty and political corruption that afflicted the nation. "The rise of large-scale corporations was unsettling, even frightening," writes one scholar.

> United States Steel, Standard Oil, and the rest were certainly remarkable creations [and] they provided a host of new goods and services, often at lower costs. . . . [But] they wielded disturbing economic power: more than one industry had become an oligopoly, basically controlled by a handful of large firms. The corporations could hurt consumers by raising the price of goods; they could hurt farmers and businessmen by raising railroad rates and hiking the cost of raw materials; they could hurt workers by cutting wages and demanding more productivity; they could hurt competitors by slashing the price of finished products and raising the price of raw materials; they could hurt towns, cities, whole regions of the country by manipulating freight charges and putting railroads and factories in one locale or another.[41]

This unhappiness with the direction of American society became so profound that lawmakers finally responded. They passed laws designed to curb the power of the country's corporate giants and address the festering social problems created by industrialization. "The captains of industry who have driven the railway systems across this continent, who have built up our commerce, who have developed our manufactures, have on the whole done great good to our people," admitted President Theodore Roosevelt in 1903. "Yet it is also true that there are real and great evils [in corporate America] . . . and a resolute and practical effort must be made to correct these evils."[42]

From the 1890s through 1920, numerous laws were passed at the city, state, and federal level to reduce the influence of big business and increase the rights of workers. Some of these laws were ineffective, but others did reduce exploitation of workers, help the elderly, decrease the use of child labor, and eliminate business monopolies in certain industries. And all of this legislation ushered in a new chapter in American history; from this point forward, the U.S. government has taken a much more active role in regulating business activity and treating social problems.

Gender Roles and Women's Rights

The industrial revolution also triggered major changes in the lives of American women. Prior to industrialization, the work necessary to thrive in America's farming-oriented economy had been carried out by both men and women. Certainly, some chores and duties were divided based on gender. Men had greater responsibility for field work, while women spent more of their time tending to housework and child rearing. Nonetheless, husbands and wives generally worked as a team to make their farms successful, and they often saw each other over the course of a day.

As the industrial revolution swept across the United States during the nineteenth century, however, this situation changed. Large numbers of families left rural America for the fast-growing cities. Once they settled in to these cities, men took factory jobs and women were left to take care of the children and the numerous household chores associated with nineteenth-century life. Some young women entered the industrial world as well—most visibly in the New England textile mills—but they were generally segregated from male workers, and they often left these jobs once they were married and started families.

By the mid-nineteenth century, industrialization had expanded the need for clerks, managers, engineers, and skilled craftsmen, all of whom became members of the nation's ever-growing middle class. Men almost always filled these positions, leaving their wives with more leisure time than ever before. Yet women's opportunities for personal growth were in some ways more limited than ever before. The men who dominated America's industrializing society came to view the home as a sanctuary from the factory floors and corporate offices in which they toiled. They made it clear that they wanted their wives and daughters to devote their energies and talents to home and hearth and leave the messy arenas of business and politics to men. In this culture, the most highly prized women were those who displayed good manners, high morals, and docile obedience to husbands and fathers.

Some women, though, openly rebelled at these restrictions. They wanted to end their exclusion from the exciting new business world that industrialization had created. They also wanted increased access to higher education and greater freedom to make their own life choices and their own judgments about "moral" and "appropriate" behavior. Finally, they wanted more of a voice in America's political life. They knew that if they had suffrage—the right to vote—then issues and causes that were important to them would get more attention.

All of these factors contributed to sustained campaigns for suffrage and women's rights in the second half of the nineteenth century. The birth of the

The women's suffrage movement can be traced back to leaders Elizabeth Cady Stanton (left) and Susan B. Anthony.

Suffrage Champion Alice Paul

A lice Paul was born on January 11, 1885, in Moorestown, New Jersey. As Paul grew up, her Quaker parents instilled in her a strong sense of social justice and a deep belief in woman suffrage. After earning a master's degree in sociology at the University of Pennsylvania in 1907, Paul went to England to study and pursue social work. Soon after her arrival, though, she became an activist for the Women's Social and Political Union (WSPU), an aggressive organization that was fighting for woman suffrage in Great Britain.

In 1910 Paul returned to the United States, where she established herself as one of the nation's most outspoken champions of women's voting rights. Paul founded the National Woman's Party in 1916. This organization quickly became well known for its confrontational tactics and passionate membership. Paul organized hunger strikes and protests in front of the White House. She was arrested and jailed on several occasions for these activities, but historians believe that her activism helped convince President Woodrow Wilson to publicly support suffrage in 1918.

In 1920 the Nineteenth Amendment to the Constitution granting women the right to vote was ratified and became law. With this victory under her belt, Paul moved on to become a leading women's rights advocate on other issues. She also became a prominent peace activist in the 1930s and 1940s. Paul died on July 9, 1977.

women's movement in America is usually traced to an 1848 convention at Seneca Falls, New York, that was organized by Lucretia Mott and Elizabeth Cady Stanton. At first, the movement was ridiculed or ignored. But time and time again activists successfully framed the issue of suffrage as one of basic justice. "It was we, the people" who were cited in the U.S. Constitution, declared the famous suffragist Susan B. Anthony. "Not we, the white male citizens; nor yet we, the male citizens; but we, the whole people, who formed the Union. And we formed it, not to give the blessings of liberty, but to secure them; not to the half of ourselves and the half of our posterity, but to the whole people—women as well as men."[43]

Public support for suffrage and women's rights strengthened throughout the last decades of the nineteenth century. The battle continued in the early twentieth century under a new generation of leaders like Alice Paul and Carrie Chapman Catt. On August 26, 1920, the right to vote was finally extended to American women when the Nineteenth Amendment became part of the U.S. Constitution.

The Dawning of Public Education

The industrial revolution also had a significant impact on the American education system. Prior to the 1830s a public school system did not exist in the United States. Formal schooling was not even available in some parts of the country, and children of wealthy families received far greater levels of instruction (often from private tutors) than did children from poor, working-class, or even middle-class backgrounds.

In the 1830s and 1840s, though, New England reformers began calling for the establishment of free public schools across the country. Despite the fact that these schools would be paid for through higher taxes, major manufacturing companies were among the most enthusiastic supporters of the idea. Their influence with lawmakers made passage of laws

Iowa schoolchildren attending the sixth grade in 1910. Prior to the 1830s, a public school system did not exist in the United States.

supporting public schools more likely. "Enlightened self-interest, another name for corporate social responsibility, guided [the corporations]," explains one historian. Corporate owners reasoned that "a literate and numerate work force would be more productive than an ignorant one. . . . The school would inculcate [instill] habits of punctuality, self-discipline, and obedience to authority."[44]

In 1852 Massachusetts passed the nation's first mandatory school attendance laws. Many other states quickly followed suit, although it was not until 1918 that all states had such laws in place. During the second half of the nineteenth century, state legislatures also moved to provide funding for public schools for all American children. By the end of the nineteenth century, free elementary public school systems were in place in every state. In 1925, though, Catholic opposition to public schooling led to a U.S. Supreme Court ruling that permitted parents to enroll children in private schools. This mix of public and private elementary and high school systems remains in place today.

Early Outlines of Modern Daily Life

Other glimmers of daily life as we know it today also began to take shape across America during the nineteenth century. And as with so many other aspects of American existence in that century, the industrial revolution played an important role in that transformation.

For example, industrialization transformed the infrastructure of American society.

Sewer systems, gaslight-illuminated streets, public transit systems (in the form of streetcars), skyscrapers, luxury liners, and sophisticated waterworks all became realities during this era. In addition, technology made homes more comfortable than ever before. By the 1850s, for example, many homes of the wealthy and middle-class were outfitted with central heating and gaslight fixtures.

Advances in communication and transportation, meanwhile, opened new worlds of opportunity, recreation, and adventure for Americans. "Before the early nineteenth century . . . people seldom ventured more than fifty miles from where they had been born, or, if they did, never saw their birthplace again," observes one historian.

Now, in less than a lifetime, it had become possible to travel a hundred miles in a day, receive instant word from someone a thousand miles away, and read of events that were taking place, right then, halfway around the world. It was possible to have hot water run out of a tap, be warm on the coldest night, read a book at night without eyestrain. These miracles of daily life that piled one upon the other in the first decades of the nineteenth century . . . induced a mood of optimism and a belief in progress that had not been known before.[45]

The industrialization of the United States also created an increasingly consumer-oriented society. Many Americans did not have the economic resources to take part

During the early 1900s, famous retail stores such as Macy's (pictured here) began to emerge in large cities like New York City.

in this transition. But those who did have the money rushed to purchase the wide array of products available in the new industrial America. They bought processed foods, decorative furniture, household cleaning products, toys and games, ready-made clothing for work and play, and countless other goods that had not existed in large quantities a half century earlier. By the 1890s big department stores and other mass retail outlets were sprouting across the country. Many famous names in American retail business history, such as Woolworth's, Macy's, Marshall Field, and Sears & Roebuck, emerged during this period.

America's First Sports Star

John L. Sullivan was the last and most famous of the "bare-knuckle" prizefighting champions in boxing's pre–glove era. Born in Roxbury, Massachusetts, on October 15, 1858, Sullivan entered the world of prizefighting in his teens. By the late 1870s he was known in many parts of the country for his fistfighting skills.

No formal boxing titles existed in Sullivan's time, but boxing historians agree that he was the foremost heavyweight boxer in America—and possibly the world—from the early 1880s through 1892, when he lost to "Gentleman" Jim Corbett in a celebrated match. During his reign as the unofficial heavyweight champion of the world, Sullivan became a celebrity. But newspaper coverage of the era often painted him as little more than an alcoholic lout, so he was both loved and hated by American boxing fans.

After losing to Corbett, Sullivan's fame quickly faded. He supported himself by touring on the vaudeville circuit, but he was virtually forgotten until 1905, when he announced that he had sworn off alcohol and become a temperance activist. "As a crusader against alcohol, Sullivan at last found a way to redeem his public image," wrote historian Wells Twombly. "His role as temperance leader may have been no closer to the inner man than the role of prizefighter, but at least it was a more serene one. It repaid him with a little of the peace he had lost in becoming the first superstar, the first personality to overwhelm his sport and the public."

Source: Wells Twombly, *200 Years of Sport in America: A Pageant of a Nation at Play.* New York: McGraw-Hill, 1976.

John L. Sullivan was the last heavyweight prizefighter not to use gloves during matches.

Bicycles and other sports equipment were also popular with American consumers during the final decades of the nineteenth century. Their popularity reflected the nation's growing appetite for leisure and recreational activities. Musicals, vaudeville shows, circuses, and other forms of live entertainment drew huge audiences of paying customers, and sports such as football and basketball burst into the nation's consciousness during this time as well. Other competitive sports, such as bike racing and wrestling, also caught the fancy of wage-earning Americans. The public's passion for sports became so great that the most noted athletes of the era, such as boxer John L. Sullivan, ranked as actual celebrities.

The rise of sports in American culture was due in large part to the increases in leisure time and discretionary income that came to many Americans after industrialization. But the popularity of sports and recreation also reflected growing American confidence in itself at century's end. "It was a time of trumpets and drums," explains one historian. "America sensed that she was an emerging power, and she strutted furiously before the rest of the world. . . . America was captivated by any sport that might glorify it."[46]

Chapter Five

Revolutionary Changes in the New Century

The industrial revolution entered a new and exciting phase in the early twentieth century. At this time, amazing new machines like the telephone, the automobile, and the airplane became fixtures in the nation's culture and economy. These inventions, combined with technological advances in numerous other industries, transformed daily life for Americans in all sorts of ways. In addition, the economic development that accompanied these innovations lifted the United States to a place of unquestioned economic dominance in the world.

The Telegraph Gives Way to the Telephone

One of the most important inventions that changed American business and culture in the twentieth century—the telephone—had actually been introduced in the 1870s. But Alexander Graham Bell's invention did not replace the telegraph

as the nation's leading communication tool until the early 1900s.

In its earliest decades, the telephone industry was dominated by the Bell Telephone Company and its long-distance service subsidiary, American Telephone & Telegraph (AT&T). This monopoly was short-lived, though. Bell remained the industry's giant, but by 1900 more than six thousand companies were supplying service to 1.4 million telephone owners across the country. The smaller independent companies could not compete with Bell in the big cities, but they prospered in more rural areas of the country.

These smaller firms were able to survive because of steadily rising demand for the telephone. Indeed, Bell's invention swept across the country with amazing speed. By 1910, 7.5 million telephones were in service, and in the early 1920s the number of telephones installed in American homes and businesses passed the 15 million mark.[47] After all, the benefits of

Telephone operators work the switchboard at the Cortlandt Telephone Exchange in New York City in 1901. It was not until the early 1900s that the telephone began to replace the telegraph as the preferred communication device of Americans.

the telephone were clear to virtually everyone. It greatly aided business enterprises and government agencies alike, and it enabled people to converse with friends and families who lived far away. The telephone was particularly treasured in rural communities because it helped ward off feelings of isolation and loneliness that haunted many farming families.

The telephone was not universally loved, however. A few observers expressed concern that the telephone—along with other new innovations like the streetcar and the automobile—were eroding traditional community ties. "In our own life," wrote sociologist Charles Horton Cooley in 1912, "the intimacy of the neighborhood has been broken up by the growth of an intricate mesh of wider contacts which leaves us strangers to people who live in the same house . . . diminishing our economic and spiritual community with our neighbors."[48]

These concerns, though, were drowned out by the enthusiasm that most Americans felt for the new device. During the 1920s and 1930s the telephone industry continued to grow, defying the economic downturn of the Great Depression. During this time AT&T (which had become the parent company to the Bell System in 1899) reestablished its monopoly power over the industry, and the network became more sophisticated and far-reaching with every passing year. By 1940 the company had not only established phone service to most American homes and businesses, it had also opened transatlantic service (in 1927) and transpacific service (in 1934). "From

World War I to 1940," writes one historian, "competition almost ceased as the companies divided the telephone business among themselves under the [control] of AT&T and the supervision of federal and state regulators. The telephone system remained essentially the same as it was on the eve of World War II until the court-ordered dismemberment of AT&T forty-four years later."[49]

The Golden Age of Radio

Wireless broadcast radio was another major milestone of the industrial revolution. This breakthrough in communications technology gave American business an exciting new avenue through which it could advertise its products and services. It also ushered in a new era in popular entertainment and became a centerpiece of American family life throughout the first half of the twentieth century.

The first experiments in harnessing radio waves for long-distance communication were made by late-nineteenth-century inventors and scientists like Guglielmo Marconi and Nikola Tesla. During the 1900s and 1910s European and American engineers and entrepreneurs built on their work, refining the technology and experimenting with various ways to harness radio's possibilities for profit. But it was not until the early 1920s that commercial radio broadcasting became a reality. In 1920 KDKA, based in Pittsburgh, Pennsylvania, became the first U.S.-licensed general radio broadcasting station in America. Twenty-five more stations were licensed in 1921,

Broadcasters work at Pittsburgh radio station KDKA in the 1920s. KDKA was the first U.S.-licensed general radio broadcasting station in the country.

and more than six hundred in 1922, including seventy-four operated by colleges and universities.

The 1920s were years of general economic prosperity and optimism in the United States, and many Americans came to view radio—along with the automobile—as one of the most potent symbols of this miraculous new age. American families loved the fact that they could now receive live musical performances, sporting events, comedy shows, news headlines, and all sorts of other entertainment in their living rooms with the click of a dial, and they rushed to purchase radio sets and equipment from local stores. An estimated 2 million radio sets were sold across the United States in 1925 alone. By the end of that year one out of every six homes in America featured a radio. And as historians Robert Hilliard and Michael Keith noted, the new technology quickly supplanted newspapers as the country's preferred source of news and entertainment:

> The prosperity and brashness of the Roaring Twenties, including the increasing domination of big business, gave importance to radio's livetime national advertising potentials. By and large, it was a time of affluence and material possessions, the growth of a new economic middle class, new opportunities through mass production for unskilled and skilled workers, and a national devil-may-care euphoria. Radio fit perfectly into this heady postwar world, sometimes informing, sometimes educating, sometimes assuaging, and mostly entertaining.[50]

The leading radio broadcasters in this era were the Columbia Broadcasting System (CBS) and the National Broadcasting Company (NBC), both of which developed impressive national networks of local radio stations. These networks became even more valuable after passage of the Radio Act of 1927. This legislation created the Federal Radio Commission (FRC) to oversee and regulate all aspects of broadcasting. For NBC, CBS, and other industry participants, however, the most essential duty of the FRC was to assign specific radio frequencies to individual stations. This change brought much-needed order to the air waves, for the number of radio stations had grown so quickly that the entire industry had been in danger of choking itself to death in a blizzard of competing radio signals.

As it turned out, though, broadcast radio's reign as America's leading source of news and entertainment would be a short one. Radio continues to exist, of course, as a popular source of music, entertainment, and news, and millions of people still listen to commercial or satellite radio on a daily basis. But in the 1950s a new communications medium called television arrived—and American business and society were changed forever.

Television in America

The earliest television technology grew out of the work of numerous inventors, scientists, and engineers at the beginning of the twentieth century. But the first working electronic television systems did not appear until the 1920s. At that time the CBS and NBC radio networks took the lead in pursuing commercial applications for this dawning technology. Several executives and inventors provided vital contributions to television technology during this time, including Philo Farnsworth and Vladimir Zworykin.

But perhaps no one was as important to the industry's development as David Sarnoff, who headed the Radio Corporation of America (RCA), the parent company of NBC. Sarnoff was convinced that television was the world's next great leap in communication, and he worked tirelessly to see his vision become a reality. "[Television] is a new art so important in its implications that it is bound to affect all of society," he declared in 1939. "It is an art which shines like a torch of hope

David Sarnoff (right), the founder of RCA, makes a statement during the opening of the 1939 New York World's Fair, the first time a news event was ever covered by television.

Revolutionary Changes in the New Century ■ 75

in the troubled world. It is a creative force which we must learn to utilize for the benefit of all mankind. This miracle of engineering skill which one day will bring the world to the home also brings a new American industry to serve man's material welfare."[51]

In 1931 CBS became the first radio network to launch experimental television broadcasts, and NBC followed one year later. These early efforts were largely ignored. The Great Depression of the 1930s seriously dampened public interest in the new technology, and military appropriations during World War II brought almost all television manufacturing and broadcasting activity to a halt. After the war, though, American households found themselves floating on a postwar wave of sustained economic prosperity. Armed with good-paying jobs—and eager to put memories of the Depression and the war behind them—American families marched to buy televisions in

Television's "Big Three"

Today, American television features dozens of cable and satellite network channels, as well as commercial-free networks like HBO. But from the 1950s through the 1970s, virtually all television programming came from three broadcast networks of allied local stations. These networks—CBS, NBC, and ABC—all began as radio networks. The Columbia Broadcasting System (CBS) was formed in 1927 through the merger of United Independent Broadcasters, a radio broadcasting company, and the Columbia Phonograph Company. The National Broadcasting Corporation (NBC) had been launched one year earlier by RCA, one of the nation's largest radio manufacturers. NBC was the industry leader for more than fifteen years. It grew so large, in fact, that it divided itself into two radio networks, called Red and Blue. In 1943, though, concerns about NBC's growing industry monopoly led the U.S. government to force NBC to sell off its Blue network. This network became the basis for the American Broadcasting Company (ABC).

Thanks to their years of operation in the radio industry, the "Big Three" networks had the best communication technology, news organizations, and stables of entertainers when television broadcasting came of age in the 1950s. Armed with these assets, they easily took control of American television. Public television stations and a small number of independent stations operated as well, but neither of these types of stations had the financial resources to compete with the big networks. As a result, the "Big Three" divided up virtually all American viewers until the 1970s, when new technology enabled cable television stations to emerge on the scene.

spectacular numbers. Television ownership jumped from 10 percent of American homes in 1950 to 87 percent by 1960. The introduction of color television sets gave another big boost to television's popularity, and by the early 1970s half of the nation's sets were color.

In 1961 government official Newton J. Minow delivered a famous speech in which he told television broadcasters that they had created a "vast wasteland" that emphasized mindless entertainment at the expense of programming that could create informed and responsible citizens. Thirty-five years later, Minow charged that little had changed.

> Every day, all across the United States, a parade of louts, losers, and con men whom most people would never allow in their homes enter anyway, through television. And every day the strangers spend more time with America's children than teachers do, or even in many cases the parents themselves. . . . No other major democratic nation in the world has so willingly turned its children over to mercenary strangers this way. No other democratic nation has so willingly converted its children into markets for commercial gain and ignored their moral, intellectual, and social development.[52]

Today, more than a half century after it first burst onto the cultural scene, television remains an influential presence in the lives of nearly all Americans. It remains a major source of information and entertainment and has long ranked as the business world's leading medium for marketing products and services to consumers. But many Americans worry that television programming has done long-lasting damage to American culture and society. These critics acknowledge that some television programs are educational and worthwhile. But they assert that much of the content that is broadcast into American homes promotes unhealthy attitudes toward sexuality and violence, and that selfish and immoral behavior is often celebrated over the airwaves.

America on Wheels

The third major innovation that transformed American business and society in the early twentieth century was the automobile. This industry sprouted out of Detroit, Michigan, in the opening years of the century, and by the 1910s it was clear that this revolutionary new invention was becoming part of the fabric of American life. From 1900 to 1910 alone, the total number of cars produced in the United States jumped from 4,000 to 187,000.[53]

Numerous automobiles were unveiled during this period by hundreds of small automobile companies. The single most influential automobile in America, though, was the Model T, which was introduced by Henry Ford in 1908. Reliable and affordable, the Model T (also known as the "Tin Lizzy") ushered in the Age of the Automobile across the United States. By 1920 Ford's vehicle accounted for 60 percent of the motor vehicles in the country.

Revolutionary Changes in the New Century ■ 77

Henry Ford's Model T ushered in America's Automobile Age, and by the 1920s accounted for 60 percent of the cars found in the United States.

This stunning success also made Ford one of the most admired individuals in the history of American business. "Opinion polls in the 1920s ranked Henry Ford just behind Jesus and Napoleon in the public's estimation of the greatest men in history," stated historian Jack Beatty. "Ford was the embodiment of enterprise, vision, and mechanical invention. . . . The conquest of American space begun by the railroad was completed by the automobile, which opened vistas not only of geography and mobility but of privacy and escape. More than any other inventor, more than any artist, writer, or politician, Henry Ford made American dreams come true.[54]

The rapid spread of the automobile was greatly aided by the introduction of credit purchasing plans. These plans also gave Americans greater ability to buy refrigerators, vacuum cleaners, radios, hair dryers, and other goods powered by electricity, which was fast becoming a standard feature in American homes and businesses. But credit plans were particularly important to the growth of the automobile industry since the purchase of an automobile—even the beloved Model T—involved a considerable outlay of money.

By the end of the 1920s there was approximately one motor vehicle for every six people in the United States. In 1929 alone, more than 5.33 million passenger cars, buses, and trucks were sold across the country. This growth not only reflected American enthusiasm for the freedom that these cars provided, but also the rising importance of car and truck transportation to other industries.

The high demand for automobiles also prompted the industry to make its operations ever more efficient and profitable. Alfred Sloan's reorganization of the administration of General Motors in the 1920s was a particularly momentous event for American business and industry. Sloan changed the company from a loose collection of affiliated companies with blurred lines of accountability and supervision into streamlined divisions that had power to quickly respond to changing market conditions—but which also had to operate within policies set out by a powerful board of managers. He also introduced stunningly successful

Henry Ford and the Model T

Famed automaker Henry Ford was born in Dearborn, Michigan, in 1863. He studied and worked to be an engineer, and in the early 1890s he took a job with Thomas Edison's Detroit Illuminating Company. During this time Ford began experimenting with automobile designs, and by the end of the century he had built several working prototypes. These successes attracted the attention of investors, and in 1903 he launched the Ford Motor Company.

In 1908 Ford unveiled a new automobile called the Model T, which still ranks as the most famous and influential automobile in the history of the industry. Ford was able to sell the reliable Model T at a price that attracted middle-class buyers because his introduction of the moving assembly line kept production costs low. Ford's assembly line was quickly adopted by other industries, and it remains a hallmark of modern industrial manufacturing.

Ford built an automotive empire during the 1910s and 1920s, and his 1914 decision to pay his workers five dollars a day—a very high wage for the era—further bolstered his reputation across America as one of its finest citizens. He also was a generous philanthropist who established hospitals and charitable foundations that exist today. As time passed, though, Ford's reputation as a hero of the industrial age was tarnished by exposure of his anti-Semitic views, his controlling attitude toward his company's workforce, and his ruthless attempts to stifle labor unions. In 1945 Ford turned over the reins of the company to his grandson, Henry Ford II, and retired. He died at his Dearborn estate in 1947.

new marketing strategies, such as modest changes in the appearance of automobile models from year to year. These cosmetic changes cost General Motors relatively little money, but they attracted millions of customers who wanted to make sure that they had the most recent model parked in their driveway. All in all, Sloan's triumphant "Management Revolution" not only vaulted General Motors to the top of the industry in the 1930s, it also changed the way that numerous other industries arranged their operations.

Meanwhile, automobile manufacturing needs provided a lucrative new market for a wide range of industries. By the end of the 1920s, for example, carmakers were consuming about 10 percent of the nation's hardwood, 15 percent of its iron and steel, and 85 percent of its rubber. The industry also prompted new waves of road and highway construction, commercial development, and residential housing construction across the country. Finally, automobile owners needed gasoline to run their machines, so they became the leading source of income for oil producers.[55]

The Great Depression of the 1930s took a heavy toll on American automakers. But heavy demand for planes, tanks, clothing, food, and other goods during World War II got American factories roaring again. When the United States emerged from the war in 1945 it slipped into a period of general economic prosperity that lasted through the 1950s. Ford Motor Company, General Motors, and the Chrysler Corporation—the so-called "Big Three" of U.S. automakers—reaped the benefits of the surging economy. In the decade after World War II, the number of passenger cars on American roads doubled, from 24 million to 48 million. The profits of oil companies jumped at this time as well, as gasoline consumption soared all over the country.

The mid-century growth of America's oil companies provided a clear example of the importance of the U.S. auto industry to the nation's overall economic health. When automakers suffered downturns in sales, the ripples were felt in numerous other industries. But when America's automobile manufacturers thrived, the entire economy benefited. "If any industry represented America's industrial might in the twentieth century, surely it was auto makers," states one historian. "The handful of companies clustered around Detroit produced the assembly line in 1913, tanks and aircraft engines during World War II, and thousands of high-paying factory jobs when peace came. The industry became the backbone of the U.S. economy and its companies America's bellwethers. As cars went, so went the nation."[56]

A New Industry Takes Wing

The last chapter in the industrial revolution's makeover of the world of transportation was written by the inventors and entrepreneurs who brought the airplane to life. For centuries, people across the globe had dreamed of finding a way to take flight into the skies. But it was not until December 17, 1903, that this dream became a reality. On that day, brothers Orville and Wilbur Wright became airborne in a motor-powered glider for a

The Wright Brothers and the Age of Flight

Aviation pioneers Orville and Wilbur Wright were born into a Midwestern farming family in post–Civil War America. Wilbur was born on April 16, 1867, in Millville, Indiana, while Orville was born on August 19, 1871, in Dayton, Ohio. In 1892 the brothers opened a bicycle shop in Dayton, and over the next few years they began manufacturing their own bikes for sale. During this same period, they began following the progress of several European inventors who were experimenting with gliders as a vehicle for manned flight. Wilbur even struck up a friendly correspondence with French glider expert Octave Chanute, who encouraged the Wright brothers when they began conducting their own glider experiments.

From 1900 to 1902 the Wright brothers worked exhaustively on various kite and glider designs. In 1903 their efforts paid off when they made the first airplane flight at Kitty Hawk, North Carolina. Two years later the Wrights built an airplane that could remain airborne for more than a half hour, and in 1908 Orville made the world's first flight of over one hour at a demonstration for U.S. Army officials at Fort Myer, Virginia. That same year, Wilbur piloted more than one hundred flights in France.

Around this time, though, the Wrights became entangled in legal battles with plane manufacturers whom the brothers charged with violating their design patents. Then, in May 1912 Wilbur died from a bout with typhoid fever. Orville gave up flying a few years later, and he spent the rest of his life as a flight researcher and designer of aeronautical equipment. He died of a heart attack on January 30, 1948.

The Wright brothers' first flight at Kitty Hawk, North Carolina, on December 17, 1903.

twelve-second flight covering 120 feet (36.6m) at Kitty Hawk, North Carolina.

Remarkably, this momentous ride did not attract a great deal of public attention when it occurred. But over the next few years, the Wright brothers and various American and European inventors made a flurry of important technological advances. Still U.S. industry and government remained strangely disinterested in the invention until World War I. At that time European aircraft came to play such an important role in the conflict that American officials and investors finally roused themselves to action. During and after the war, America began to invest much more heavily in the new industry. The U.S. Post Office introduced airmail service between Washington, D.C., and New York in 1918, and the U.S. military began acquiring airplanes in greater and greater numbers. This market gave a much-needed boost to early American aircraft makers.

The commercial potential of airplanes, meanwhile, became evident in May 1927, when American aviator Charles Lindbergh completed a flight from New York to Paris, France, over the course of two days. This feat made Lindbergh an international hero and convinced investors and ordinary Americans alike that long-distance flight could one day stand as a safe way to travel long distances. It also gave additional momentum to governmental efforts to implement rules and safeguards for the fast-growing industry. By the end of the 1920s, both airplanes and pilots were subject to a number of licenses and operating regulations. In addition, the U.S. government passed laws that enabled private carriers to deliver mail. This became an important source of income for America's first generation of air carriers.

In the 1930s American and European aircraft continued to get bigger, stronger, and faster. Advances in engine and propeller design, landing gear, navigation instruments, and wing design made airplanes more efficient than ever before. These innovations proved vital during World War II, when American air power helped the Allies defeat Nazi Germany and Japan. By the time the war ended in 1945, jet-powered engines were ready for implementation not only in military aircraft, but also in the business and travel sectors of the industry.

During the 1950s and 1960s advances in aeronautics came so fast and furious that new technological marvels seemed to appear with each passing month. Supersonic flights, guided missiles, space satellites, and manned rockets designed for space exploration all burst out of the world of science fiction to become daily realities. Much of the investment and research that made these marvels possible stemmed from the ongoing "Cold War," a four-decade-long economic and military rivalry between the United States and the Soviet Union that began immediately after World War II. During this same era, commercial air travel continued to grow by leaps and bounds. By the mid-1970s nearly 13,000 airports dotted the landscape of America, including more than 450 that featured regularly scheduled airline service.

America's Consumer Economy

The manufacturers and carriers who comprised the commercial air travel industry in America were successful for the same reason that other U.S. manufacturers and retail businesses thrived: Steady industrial and economic expansion had transformed the people of the United States into the greatest consumers of goods and services on the planet. The broad outlines of this modern consumer economy had become visible as early as the Roaring Twenties. But the consumer economy did not truly arrive until the 1950s and 1960s. In these decades—which were marked by the introduction of shopping malls, credit cards, and other familiar elements of modern consumerism—America became a nation of shoppers.

In the years following World War II, the surging economic power of the United States was plain to everyone. As the business magazine *Fortune* declared in June 1953,

Customers crowd the television department of a Polk Brothers store in 1954. Business used the emerging medium of television as its primary tool to market its goods and services to American consumers.

All history can show no more portentous economic phenomenon than today's American market. It is colossal, soaking up half the world's steel and oil and three-fourths of its cars and appliances. The whole world fears it and is baffled by it. Let U.S. industry slip 5 percent, and waves of apprehension sweep through foreign chancelleries. Let U.S. consumer spending lag even half as much, and the most eminent economists anxiously read the omens. The whole world also marvels at and envies this market. It is enabling Americans to raise their standard of living every year while other countries have trouble in maintaining theirs. And of course the whole world wants to get in on it. For it still can punish the incompetent and inefficient, and still reward handsomely the skillful, efficient, and daring.[57]

This sustained economic "boom" was driven by a multitude of factors, not just one event or invention. Increased access to government loans, expanded credit, longer shopping hours, new housing and other development associated with suburbanization, and the introduction of shopping malls all contributed to what some critics called "affluenza"—excessive consumer consumption. But as one history of U.S. consumerism noted, "perhaps no single cause was as responsible for the emerging postwar epidemic of affluenza than the ubiquitous box that found its way into most American homes by the 1950s."[58] This box—television—became the primary means by which American industry marketed its goods and services to consumers. And it helped breed an appetite for acquiring everything from automobiles to appliances to beauty products. By 1970, for example, Americans were spending four times as much shopping as Europeans.[59]

Some critics have charged that American consumer spending has gotten out of control in the last half century. They assert that Americans have become excessively materialistic and that their heavy levels of consumption have become a threat to the planet's limited natural resources. They also charge that Americans spend so much on unnecessary or even frivolous goods and services that they jeopardize their own long-term economic security. But others defend American spending habits. They state that consumers should not have to apologize for providing a comfortable, enjoyable living environment for themselves and their families. Meanwhile, even as this debate has intensified, the nation's consumer economy has continued to grow by leaps and bounds, carrying American business and industry into the twenty-first century.

Chapter Six

Industry and Technology in the Modern Era

The modern world in which we live today bears little resemblance to the world that existed in the days of Robert Fulton, Thomas Edison, Eli Whitney, John D. Rockefeller, and other legends of American business history. Yet contemporary America owes its current character to the industrial revolution. Many of the inventions that washed across the United States and Europe in the nineteenth and early twentieth centuries are still integral parts of American society. Automobiles and airplanes remain the most popular means by which people travel, telephones remain a fixture in the daily lives of virtually all citizens, and machine-oriented factories, refineries, and shipyards remain important employers and centers of economic activity in many American communities.

Other American industries that were important factors in the industrial revolution, though, are far less influential than they once were. Most textile manufacturing, for example, now takes place overseas, and the telegraph has long since given way to electronic mail, cellular telephones, and other tools of modern communication technology. A century ago, railroads were the single most important element in the country's swift economic and geographic expansion, but today they only play a minor role in U.S. business. These developments show that the American economy—and the many industries that comprise that economy—now exists in an era of rapid technological, political, and cultural change. Together, these forces continue to change the face of American business and industry on a daily basis.

The Changing Face of American Industry

American business at the beginning of the twenty-first century is different in many important ways than it was a hundred

With the support of politicians like Franklin Roosevelt, labor unions grew during the first half of the twentieth century.

years ago. Industrial pollution and excessive consumption of natural resources have been linked to global warming, species loss, and other serious environmental problems in the United States and around the world. This knowledge has prompted heated debates over the best ways to balance economic growth and environmental stewardship. Government regulation and oversight of U.S. business has also increased, driven by concerns about workplace safety, fair treatment of employees, and the financial security of workers who retired or are injured on the job. And industries in the United States and around the world are grappling with growing evidence that world supplies of oil—the primary fuel of the Industrial Age—are being exhausted at a frightening rate. This prospect has led to the emergence of whole new industries devoted to finding alternative energy sources.

Changing Fortunes

The picture of the typical American worker has also changed dramatically over the past century. During the first half of the twentieth century, unionization of the American work force increased at a steady rate. At the height of the Great Depression in the mid-1930s, union membership stood at only 3 million members. But general economic prosperity, talented and dedicated union leadership, and the support of politicians like Franklin D. Roosevelt boosted the fortunes of the United Auto Workers and a host of other labor organizations. By 1945, 12 million American workers held union memberships, primarily in man-

ufacturing industries. In 1953 the number of union members reached nearly 17 million, about 28 percent of the total U.S. work force.[60] But since 1979, when the number of American union workers reached a peak of 21 million, union membership has declined significantly. By 2003 union membership had fallen to 15.8 million workers, about 11.5 percent of the American workforce.[61]

A leading factor in the declining influence of organized labor has been the steady shift of numerous manufacturing jobs from American soil to foreign countries. Advances in transportation, communication, and other technology areas have enabled "multinational" corporations—businesses with interests in countries all around the globe—to move many of their factories and other operations to countries where they can pay much lower wages. Environmental and workplace regulations are also much less strict in many of these countries. In addition, international trade agreements have made it easier for these same companies to ship foreign-made goods into the United States for sale. Finally, labor unions lost political clout in many parts of the country in the 1980s, when pro-management politicians held growing influence in the White House and Congress.

These events have produced a remarkable drop in the amount of industrial manufacturing that takes place in the United States. In the late 1940s manufacturing jobs accounted for 40 percent of all U.S. jobs. By 1981, though, this percentage had dropped to 27 percent, and in 2007 only 12 percent of American jobs were in the manufacturing sector, according to the U.S. Bureau of Labor Statistics. During this same period, jobs in what is known as the "service industries"—work in restaurants, retail stores, landscaping, hotels, and other businesses that provide services rather than products to customers—have surged across the United States. Economists point out, though, that these occupations generally do not pay as well as the manufacturing jobs that are being lost overseas.

By 2004 one-third of all manufactured products sold in the United States were actually produced overseas. This trend is present in all sorts of industries, from toy manufacturing to automobile production. In 2004 about one-third of all vehicles bought in the United States were imported. In addition, about 40 percent of the parts that are used in cars built in the United States actually come from factories in Mexico and other foreign countries. Among suppliers of manufacturing technology and equipment, the drop in U.S. production is even more startling. U.S. production of machine tools fell by two-thirds between 1998 and 2004, by which time imports accounted for two-thirds of the machine tools sold in the United States. Machine tool makers in Japan, which has half the population of the United States, registered more than three times the revenue from sales in the United States as American machine tool makers.[62] Analysts believe that these trends are likely to continue without major new governmental and corporate investments in American manufacturing technology and facilities.

The so-called "global economy" of the early twenty-first century, though, has also created opportunities for some modern industries. Transportation, communications, and other high-technology industries have benefited enormously from these changes. Of these industries, the most spectacular growth has come in the computer and software industries. When commercial microprocessors—essentially tiny computers placed on silicon chips—were introduced into computers in the early 1970s, the computing power of these machines increased by leaps and bounds. In a matter of a few years, computers became essential to virtually every large business enterprise. As one scholar noted,

> The computer, like the steam engine, produced an economic revolution, and for precisely the same reason: it caused a collapse in the price of a fundamental input into the economic system, allowing that input to be applied to an infinity of tasks that previously had been too expensive or simply impossible. The steam engine brought down the price of work-doing energy; the computer brought down the price of storing, retrieving, and manipulating information.[63]

American Business in the Internet Age

The U.S. computer and software industries also owe much of their incredible growth and financial success to the Internet. This vast global communications system of interconnected computer net-

A "Second Industrial Revolution" in China

Since the 1990s the Asian nation of China has been undergoing what some economists call the "Second Industrial Revolution." During the eighteenth and nineteenth centuries, when Europe and then the United States built industry-based economies, China remained a nation of farmers with little manufacturing capacity. In the last years of the twentieth century, however, the Communist leadership of China decided to expand and modernize their economy. Their policies, combined with a huge supply of cheap labor and the existence of beneficial international trade agreements, have created an incredible explosion of building in the nation's cities. Factories, shopping centers, and office buildings have sprouted up all across China, and huge quantities of oil, iron ore, and other materials destined for manufacturers arrive at Chinese seaports every day. This economic growth has also sparked a tremendous migration of people in China—the most heavily populated country in the world—from rural areas into the industrializing cities.

These changes have made China one of the greatest economic powers in the world. But many analysts believe that the country has only tapped a fraction of its full commercial potential. In fact, economists believe that by mid century, China's economy could rival or even surpass the economy of the United States and become the most powerful one on the planet.

works was built in the 1970s and 1980s by a large community of scientists and entrepreneurs like Tim Berners-Lee, Vinton Cerf, Robert Taylor, and Steve Case. In many ways, these and other early contributors to the Internet were just as visionary as Henry Ford, Robert Fulton, and other legends of the industrial revolution. "The Internet . . . owed its exuberance and vigor to the spirit of entrepreneurs of all ages who can see a new, wide open, and limitless vista before them,"[64] writes one scholar.

Since its emergence into general use in the early 1990s, the Internet has completely changed the way that Americans—and people in many other parts of the world—conduct business, communicate with one another, and spend their free time. In fact, the Internet has become a routine part of daily life for most Americans. The changes to American business and industry in the Internet Age have been particularly dramatic. For example, this technology has made it much easier for businesses to interact with existing customers—and attract potential new customers. Web sites give businesses the power to advertise their products and services, communicate with customers,

Vinton Cerf, the "Father of the Internet"

Vinton Gray Cerf was born on July 23, 1943, in Hew Haven, Connecticut. After graduating from Stanford University he took a computer programming job with IBM, but in the early 1970s he moved on to the Advanced Research Projects Agency (ARPA), a division of the U.S. Department of Defense. At that time, the agency was working on the world's first computer network. This network, called the ARPANET, is commonly described as a forerunner of the Internet.

During the 1970s Cerf and colleagues like Robert Kahn strung together a network of computers in locations across the country. In addition, they devised complex rules or protocols for network communication. They also researched ways to connect the ARPANET to computer networks in Europe and elsewhere. These "internetworking" efforts eventually became the basis for the term "Internet."

The protocols introduced by Cerf and his fellow researchers became widely accepted in the late 1970s and early 1980s. Once computer scientists had these common rules to follow, the development of a global computer network became a much more achievable goal. Cerf remained at the forefront of these research efforts, and by the late 1980s he was widely described as the "father" of the emerging Internet.

Since that time, Cerf has remained heavily involved in Internet issues, from areas of computing technology to policy making. In 1997 he and Robert Kahn received the U.S. National Medal of Technology in recognition of their essential role in the development of the Internet.

Vinton Cerf was integral to the early stages of Internet development.

collect information about the use of their products, track inventory and shipping operations, and respond to customer feedback and changing customer tastes more quickly and efficiently than ever before.

Advances in information technology have also changed the ways in which workers interact with their employers. The capabilities of the Internet, powerful computers, and sophisticated communications devices like Blackberries permit workers to more easily work at home or other places that bear no resemblance to the traditional office environment.

Some U.S. industries have struggled to survive in this new information age. The recording industry, for example, has had to discard many of its old business practices in order to meet the demands of customers who have the capability to download billions of digital recordings from the Internet. Many record stores have been driven out of business by the changing environment as well. But other corporations from Amazon.com to eBay have risen to become economic giants strictly on the basis of Internet sales, and many other smaller companies have carved out profitable niches for themselves on the Internet. In addition, thousands of other retail and manufacturing companies have found ways to use the Internet not only for online sales but also to boost their revenue from traditional stores, shops, and manufacturing facilities.

The Future of American Business

Today, new technological innovations are being introduced into American business and society with stunning speed. Many technology experts believe that it will not be long before virtually all tools used in daily life for business and pleasure—including cars, computers, telephones, cameras, televisions, household appliances, and home security systems—will be linked together into powerful networks that users can access and control from anywhere.

But no one really knows the exact form that American business and culture will have a decade from now, let alone fifty or one hundred years in the future. "We are watching something historic happen," writes Microsoft founder Bill Gates, "and it will affect the world seismically, rocking us the same way the discovery of the scientific method, the invention of printing, and the arrival of the Industrial Age did."[65] Another observer claims that "the entire computer revolution, including the Internet, hasn't begun yet. We're not in the middle of it—we're at the dawn of it. It's like trying to comprehend the magnitude of the oceans if all you've done is stand on the beach watching the waves breaking."[66]

Whatever shape the world of business takes in the twenty-first century, though, it still has its roots in the industrial revolution. The technologically advanced global economy in which we live and work today would never have come about if it had not been for pioneering inventions like the steam engine, the cotton gin, and the telegraph. In fact, says one business scholar,

The final tally of the industrial revolution has yet to be reckoned. . . . The analysis is not simply a historical exercise, for the process is ongoing. The

Industry leaders, like Microsoft president Bill Gates, are unsure what the future of American business holds.

most fearsome toll of the industrial revolution may still await us in the form of greater environmental degradation or new kinds of conflicts between the haves and have-nots at the industrial table. Great opportunities may also beckon as various societies become increasingly able to make adjustments to the industrial world. . . . The industrial revolution, caused by an unusual set of circumstances in world history, unleashed forces that have been hard to control. The one certainty is that the process has not slowed. It continues to shape world history, from the societies seeking higher industrial achievement to societies desperately striving to preserve a newly challenged industrial lead.[67]

Notes

Introduction: One Hundred Years of Innovation

1. Peter N. Stearns, *The Industrial Revolution in World History*, 3rd ed. Boulder, CO: Westview, 2007, p. 6.
2. William Allen White, *The Autobiography of William Allen White*. New York: Macmillan, 1946, p. 390.

Chapter One: The Birthplace of the Industrial Revolution

3. Anthony Burton, *The Rise and Fall of King Cotton*. London: BBC, 1984, p. 75.
4. John Steele Gordon, *An Empire of Wealth: The Epic History of American Economic Power*. New York: Harper Collins, 2004, pp. 88–89.
5. Quoted in Manchester City Council, "Social Commentators," *Spinning the Web: The Story of the Cotton Industry*. www.spinningtheweb.org.uk.
6. Quoted in Manchester City Council, "People," *Spinning the Web: The Story of the Cotton Industry*. www.spinningtheweb.org.uk.
7. Quoted in Bruce Norman, *The Inventing of America*. London: British Broadcasting Corporation, 1976, p. 19.
8. Gordon, *Empire of Wealth*, p. 82.
9. Gordon, *Empire of Wealth*, p. 85.
10. Gordon, *Empire of Wealth*, p. 87.
11. Quoted in Stephen Yafa, *Big Cotton*. New York: Viking, 2004, p. 8.
12. Quoted in Gordon, *Empire of Wealth*, p. 89.
13. Yafa, *Big Cotton*, p. 64.

Chapter Two: The Industrial Age Transforms America

14. Quoted in Peter L. Bernstein, *Wedding of the Waters: The Erie Canal and the Making of a Great Nation*. New York: Norton, 2005, p. 343.
15. Quoted in Page Smith, *The Shaping of America*, vol. 3, *A People's History of the Young Republic*. New York: McGraw-Hill, 1980, p. 774.
16. Louis C. Hunter, *Steamboats on the Western Rivers: An Economic and Technological History*. Cambridge: Harvard University Press, 1949, p. 75.
17. Gordon, *Empire of Wealth*, p. 141.
18. Quoted in Daniel Feller, *The Jacksonian Promise: America, 1815–1840*. Baltimore: Johns Hopkins University Press, 1995, p. 25.
19. Gordon, *Empire of Wealth*, p. 137.
20. John Steele Gordon, *The Business of America: Tales from the Marketplace—American Enterprise from the Settling of New England to the Break Up of AT&T*. New York: Walker, 2001, p. 49.
21. Feller, *The Jacksonian Promise*, p. 37.
22. Feller, *The Jacksonian Promise*, p. 24.
23. Barbara Freese, *Coal: A Human History*. New York: Perseus, 2003, p. 109.
24. Freese, *Coal: A Human History*, p. 121.
25. Gordon, *Empire of Wealth*, p. 175.

Chapter Three: The "Iron Horse," the Telegraph, and Westward Expansion

26. Keith Wheeler, *The Railroaders*. New York: Time-Life Books, 1973, p. 122.
27. Quoted in Nicholas Faith, *The World the Railways Made*. New York: Carroll and Graf, 1990, p. 43.
28. Oliver Jensen, *The American Heritage History of Railroads in America*. New York: Bonanza, 1981, p. 124.
29. James A. Ward, *Railroads and the Character of America, 1820–1887*. Knoxville: University of Tennessee Press, 1986, p. 14.
30. Frederick Merk, *History of the Westward Movement*. New York: Alfred A. Knopf, 1978, p. 202.
31. Quoted in David H. Bain, *Empire Express: Building the First Transcontinental Railroad*. New York: Viking Penguin, 1999, p. 6.
32. Quoted in Ward, *Railroads and the Character of America*, p. 73.
33. Keith L. Bryant Jr., "Entering the Global Economy," *The Oxford History of the American West*, eds. Clyde A. Milner II, Carol A. O'Connor, and Martha A. Sandweiss. New York: Oxford University Press, 1994. p. 197.
34. Gordon, *Empire of Wealth*, p. 172.
35. Ron Chernow, *Titan: The Life of John D. Rockefeller, Sr.* New York: Random House, 1998, p. 249.
36. John P. Hoerr, *And the Wolf Finally Came: The Decline of the American Steel Industry*. Pittsburgh: University of Pittsburgh Press, 1988, p. 170.
37. James Howard Bridge, *The Carnegie Millions and the Men Who Made Them* (facsimile of *The Inside History of the Carnegie Steel Company: A Romance of Millions*. London: Limpus, Baker, 1903). Boston: Adamant Media, 2002, p. 169.
38. Gordon, *Empire of Wealth*, p. 149.
39. Gordon, *Empire of Wealth*, p. 153.

Chapter Four: The Economic and Social Impact of the Industrial Revolution

40. Stuart Bruchey, *The Wealth of the Nation: An Economic History of the United States*. New York: Harper & Row, 1988, p. 134.
41. Michael McGerr, *A Fierce Discontent: The Rise and Fall of the Progressive Movement in America*. New York: Oxford University Press, 2003, pp. 151–52.
42. Theodore Roosevelt, "Theodore Roosevelt: First Annual Message, December 3rd, 1901," in John T. Woolley and Gerhard Peters, *The American Presidency Project*. www.presidency.ucsb.edu/?pid=29542.
43. Quoted in Lynn Sherr, *Failure Is Impossible: Susan B. Anthony in Her Own Words*. New York: Three Rivers, 1996, pp. 110–11.
44. Merle Curti, *The Social Ideas of American Educators*. New York: Scribner's, 1935, pp. 83–84.
45. Gordon, *Empire of Wealth*, p. 163.
46. Wells Twombly, *200 Years of Sport in America: A Pageant of a Nation at Play*. New York: McGraw-Hill, 1976, p. 98.

Chapter Five: Revolutionary Changes in the New Century

47. Claude S. Fisher, *America Calling: A Social History of the Telephone to 1940*. Berkeley: University of California Press, 1992, p. 44.
48. Quoted in Fisher, *America Calling*, p. 52.

49. Fisher, *America Calling*, p. 34.

50. Robert L. Hilliard and Michael C. Keith, *The Broadcast Century and Beyond: A Biography of American Broadcasting*. 4th ed. Boston: Focal, 2004, p. 25.

51. Quoted in Marcy Carsey and Tom Werner, "Father of Broadcasting: David Sarnoff," *Time*, March 29, 1999, p. 88.

52. Newton N. Minow and Craig L. LeMay, *Abandoned in the Wasteland: Children, Television, and the First Amendment*. New York: Hill and Wang, 1996, pp. 18, 19.

53. James J. Flink, *The Automobile Age*. Cambridge, MA: MIT Press, 1988, pp. 26–27.

54. Jack Beatty, "The Business of America," in *Colossus: How the Corporation Changed America*, ed. Jack Beatty. New York: Broadway Books, 2001, pp. 256–57.

55. George S. May, *The Automobile Industry, 1920–1980*. New York: Facts On File, 1990, p. 24.

56. Joan Muller, "Autos: A New Industry," *Business Week*, July 15, 2002, p. 98.

57. Quoted in Robert Sobel, *The Great Boom*. New York: St. Martin's, 2000, p. 8.

58. John De Graaf, David Wann, and Thomas H. Naylor, *Affluenza: The All-Consuming Epidemic*. San Francisco: Berrett-Koehler, 2005, p. 145.

59. De Graaf et al., *Affluenza*, p. 145.

Chapter Six: Industry and Technology in the Modern Era

60. Daniel Nelson, *Shifting Fortunes: The Rise and Decline of American Labor, from the 1820s to the Present*. Chicago: Ivan R. Dee, 1997, p. 104.

61. Gerald Mayer, *Union Membership Trends in the United States*. Washington, DC: Congressional Research Service, August 31, 2004, p. 3.

62. Lawrence J. Rhoades, "The Transformation of Manufacturing in the 21st Century," *Bridge*, vol. 35, no. 1, spring 2005. www.nae.edu/NAE/bridge.com.

63. Gordon, *Empire of Wealth*, p. 409.

64. Quoted in Robert Sobel, *The Great Boom*. New York: St. Martin's, 2000, p. 405.

65. Bill Gates, *The Road Ahead*. New York: Penguin, 1996, p. 313.

66. Bran Ferren, "The Future of the Internet," *Discover*, November 2000.

67. Stearns, *The Industrial Revolution in World History*, p. 297.

Glossary

consumer economy: An economy in which most activity is driven by consumer purchases of goods and services.

exports: Products sent to foreign countries to be sold.

factory system: System of mass industrial production in which workers use machines to execute specialized tasks in the production process.

imports: Products created in foreign countries that are brought in for sale.

mass production: Creation of large volumes of a product through mechanization.

monopoly: Exclusive control by one company or group of companies over the sale of goods or services in a specific region.

relief: Assistance from public agencies or charitable organizations, usually in the form of money, food, or housing.

Roaring Twenties: The 1920s, a decade of general economic prosperity and growth in the United States.

robber barons: Negative nickname given to the wealthy industrialists who controlled America's leading corporations in the nineteenth and early twentieth centuries.

socialism: A social and economic system based on the collective ownership of a state's resources and the total rejection of private ownership of property and resources.

suffrage: The right to vote.

tariff: A tax on imported goods.

trust: A powerful combination of firms or companies that can manipulate or control significant aspects of an industry.

For Further Exploration

Books

Robert C. Baron, *Pioneers and Plodders: The American Industrial Spirit*. Golden, CO: Fulcrum, 2004. This book glosses over some of the problems associated with industrialization, but it does provide an interesting historical overview of business leaders in four industries: steel, automobiles, electronics, and computers.

Janet Davidson and Michael Sweeney, *On the Move: Transportation and the American Story*. Washington, DC: National Geographic Society and Smithsonian Institution, 2003. This lavishly illustrated book provides lots of fascinating information about changes in American transportation over the centuries. The book was published as a companion to a special exhibit at the National Museum of American History.

John Steele Gordon, *The Business of America: Tales from the Marketplace—American Enterprise from the Settling of New England to the Break Up of AT&T*. New York: Walker, 2001. A fast-paced but informative overview of American business history that provides lots of coverage of the industrial revolution and its economic and social impact.

———, *A Thread Across the Ocean: The Heroic Story of the Transatlantic Cable*. New York: Harper Perennial, 2003. This book details one of the great engineering feats of the industrial revolution: the construction of a communication cable across the floor of the Atlantic Ocean in order to establish telegraph service between the United States and Europe.

Oliver Jensen, *The American Heritage History of Railroads in America*. New York: Bonanza, 1981. This heavily illustrated volume traces the origins and development of American railroads. The book's coverage of the railroad's role in the development of the American West is particularly strong.

Howard Means, *Money and Power: The History of Business*. Hoboken, NJ: Wiley, 2002. A general-interest book that covers the achievements of notable individuals in world business history from ancient times to the present.

Jerry Stanley, *Big Annie of Calumet: A True Story of the Industrial Revolution*. During the American industrial revolution, bitter and sometimes violent conflicts erupted between powerful corporations and their workers. This work recounts one such clash in a Michigan mining community in the early 1900s.

Web Sites

American Experience: The Rockefellers (www.pbs.org/wgbh/amex/rockefellers/index.html). This Web site provides an overview of the life of John D. Rockefeller, perhaps the most famous industrialist in U.S. history, and his fabulously wealthy ancestors. It covers many controversies that raged during America's years of industrialization.

Biographies of the Industrial Revolution (www.42explore2.com/industrial2.htm). This Web site provides links to dozens of biographies on leading entrepreneurs, inventors, engineers, and tycoons of the industrial revolution, both in England and in the United States.

The Industrial Revolution (http://members.aol.com/TeacherNet/Industrial.html). An online clearinghouse that provides links to numerous worthwhile Web sites on various aspects of the industrial revolution.

Internet Modern History Sourcebook: The Industrial Revolution (www.fordham.edu/halsall/mod/modsbook14.html). This is another Web site that focuses on providing interested readers with lots of links to popular and academic sites covering various facets of the industrial revolution.

Railroad History Archive (http://railroads.uconn.edu/index.html). The railroad was one of the most important inventions of the entire industrial revolution, and this Web site contains a treasure trove of content about the development of the Iron Horse, as well as many worthwhile links to other railroad-related Web sites.

Index

infrastructure of, industrialization
  and development of, 66
post-Civil War crop production in, 45,
  47
steel production in, 51
westward expansion of, 44–45
U.S. Constitution, Nineteenth
  Amendment, 64

W
War of Independence, 21
Waterways, development of, 29–31
Watt, James, 19–20
Westward expansion, 44–45
Whitney, Asa, 45

Whitney, Eli, 21–22, 38
Wilson, Woodrow, 64
Women's rights, 62–64
Women's Social and Political Union
  (WSPU), 64
Workers
  exploitation of, 12, 18–19
  information technology and, 91
  lack of protections for, 58
  legislation protecting, 61–62
Wright, Orville, 80–82
Wright, Wilbur, 80–82

Z
Zworykin, Vladimir, 74

Picture Credits

Cover: Library of Congress
AP Images, 73, 75, 78, 90, 92
© Bettmann/Corbis, 8 (upper left)
© Corbis, 28, 35, 50
FPG/Getty Images, 57
Getty Images, 8 (lower left)
H.T. Cory/National Archive/Getty
　Images, 39
Hulton Archive/Getty Images, 9 (upper
　right), 16, 19, 37, 42, 52, 54, 67, 71
Kean Collection/Getty Images, 21
MPI/Getty Images, 13, 34, 43, 46, 59
Stock Montage/Getty Images, 47

Tom Stoddart/Getty Images, 9 (lower
　right)
Wallace Kirkland/Time & Life
　Pictures/Getty Images, 83
Time & Life Pictures/Mansell/Getty
　Images, 27
James Valentine/Getty Images, 18
Vintage Images/Getty Images, 65
Roger Violett/Getty Images, 31
Library of Congress, 24, 38, 63, 68, 81,
　86
National Archives and Records
　Administration, 11

About the Author

Kevin Hillstrom has written and edited numerous reference works in the areas of American history and international environmental issues. Credits include *The Cold War—Primary Sourcebook Series* (2006), the nine-volume *Industrial Revolution in America* (2005–2006), the six-volume *World's Environments* (2003–2004), and the four-volume *American Civil War Reference Library* (2000). He has also served as author or editor for ten volumes of the *Defining Moments* American history reference series.